Self Mastery
The Path to Ascension

By Peter Slattery

Self Mastery – The Path to Ascension

Self Mastery – The Path to Ascension

Copyright © 2023 by Peter Maxwell Slattery

Cover by Kesara (Christine Dennett), www.kesara.org

Editor: Jessica Bryan, www.oregoneditor.com

DISCLAIMER: The information in this book is intended to be of a general educational nature, and does not constitute medical, legal, or other professional advice for any specific individual or situation.

No part of this book may be reproduced or transmitted in any form or by any means, without permission in writing from the publisher.

The Healing Light Meditations in Chapter 4 were previously published in *MEDIUMSHIP AND THE FLOW OF GRACE* by Jessica Bryan.

Published by Peter Maxwell Slattery

Email: petermaxwellslattery@outlook.com.au

www.petermaxwellslattery.com

ISBN 978-1-4478-6138-6

Self Mastery – The Path to Ascension

I dedicate this book to you, the spiritual seeker, to the teachers, and to the many who support and are playing an active part in the healing of the Earth, humanity, and themselves, and to those who bring joy, purpose, and prosperity to all, and who contribute to the evolutionary process of humanity, Earth, and the multiverse.

A big thank you and blessings to Jessica Bryan for editing and for research, guidance, friendship, and feedback with this and my previous books.

Thank you also to Kesara (Christine Dennett) for creating the cover art.

And to my family and friends from on and off-world, as well as to the many who have offered their support.

Blessings and Jaya*

Pete

*Jaya = victory, balance of masculine, and feminine, and self-mastery in Sanskrit

Self Mastery – The Path to Ascension

WARNING

Before attempting any of the practices described in this book, set your intention and be open to experiencing that which brings joy, assists with being of service, and helps you become the best possible version of yourself.

Self Mastery – The Path to Ascension

CONTENTS

Introduction..9
Chapter 1: Upon Awakening............................15
Chapter 2: Assess and Clear...........................25
Chapter 3: Heart and Mind Coherence..............59
Chapter 4: Grounding....................................73
Chapter 5: Sensing Energy, Vibration, and Seeing the Unseen...93
Chapter 6: Manifesting................................125
Chapter 7: The Zone...................................135
Chapter 8: Witness Awareness......................151
Chapter 9: Multidimensional Vision................187
Chapter 10: The Merkabah and the Master's Journey...213
Chapter 11: Ascension and Beyond..................225
Books by Pete...231
About the Author...233
"Watching the Sky".......................................235

Self Mastery – The Path to Ascension

INTRODUCTION

Many are looking outside of themselves for answers, help, guidance, and acceptance even though everything is an aspect of God/Source/Creator and we all are Creator Beings.

Everyone needs teachers and others to learn from, to spark ideas in consciousness, and teach us techniques to help us empower ourselves. This, in effect, assists others. But the path of enlightenment, self-mastery, whatever you would like to call it, is a path like no other. If you are willing to come from a place of living in truth and excel and be the best version of yourself, as well as having discipline, it can be just a moment away.

Many are walking in darkness searching for the light, only to find that when they go within, the light has been with them all along. A whole host of guides, positive extraterrestrials, Masters, saints, and sages are ready to help you unlock your full potential.

This book includes tips and tools at the end of every chapter to guide you in living to your full potential. It is written from experience and includes stories from my journey when I was a child. It also includes some of my experiences with extraterrestrials,

Masters, Light Beings, and Source. It is impossible to cover everything, and what I am relaying here is only intended to help you connect the dots in your own life. Modify this knowledge and learn the mechanics of how the mind, body, and spirit connect to assist you with steering your human experience.

The information in this book is a template. Use it, don't use it, mix it up, spin it around, and make it work for you. As with all knowledge in the areas of spirituality, self-mastery, and the mystic journey, put it in your spiritual toolbox, so to speak.

Your mindset, focus, and goal orientation, thirst for life, service to others, growth and learning are all keys to your soul evolution, leading you ultimately to reunite with your spirit and bring clarity and direct connection to Source, God, whatever you like to call it, into your awareness. When you achieve these ideals, you will realize this connection has been there all along.

Illusionary in nature, hilarious when realized and a downright challenge, at times, the path of realization and self-mastery can lead to an experience of your true nature. Once a glimpse of this is seen by the seeker, walking in joy, compassion, love, and non-judgment of self and others comes into play and the journey truly begins.

Being almost at point X, Y, and Z since I was young, experiencing otherworldly *intelligences* (Spiritual Beings) and seeing plus knowing things others can only imagine, to later in life having the wonderment come to me about the mechanics of how we operate, our nature, and how to live to our fullest potential, I was led down a path of exploration. It wasn't about ETs or anything like that, although ET contact is a conduit to consciousness exploration. I have understood this since I was a young child, but it was the gateway that led me to delve deeper in knowing, understanding, and revelations, a foot in the door on the path to evolution.

I learned about counseling, psychology, meditation, yoga, remote-viewing, Reiki, qigong, yi-gong, and more. I became a teacher in some of these areas and received assistance from Shi-Ji the Pleiadian, Patma the Sirian, Penkay, and The Wise One from Orion, as well as the Elohim and many others on and off-world. I studied with Master James Gilliland, John Vivanco, remote viewing teacher, hypnotherapist Mary Rodwell, as well as teachers of karate (including my father) and yoga. I also learned from The Original Elders of Australia and abroad, off-world intelligences, and multidimensional masters such as Kwan Yin, Mother Mary, Baba-Ji, Ganesh, and celestial and Angelic Beings like Metatron and Archangel Michael. All these voices and more are represented here, flowing through my experience and consciousness.

The human experience is layered, convoluted, and really a cosmic joke that we play on ourselves, until we understand our true nature as we move forward in the evolution of our consciousness. This is *The Ascension,* the multidimensional process by which we increase our spiritual and energetic frequency and bring more and more Divine Light into our physical form. Eventually, we evolve into the Rainbow Body, as written about in Chapter 8.

There is much I cannot go into in this book because of the nature of some practices, plus due to all readers being at different levels of the journey, but here you will find a well-rounded range of tips and tools to help you empower yourself. They are simple, but effective. Just follow your intuition and heart and do what feels right.

When you get into the realm of initiations and certain practices, some knowledge cannot be spoken about, or the source revealed, in order to protect the integrity of the practice, and also to protect ancient knowledge from falling into the wrong hands, or into the hands of those who are not ready for the responsibility that comes with it. In addition, initiations and some practices need to be done in person.

This is a practical guide to give you an idea of how structure, spiritual practices, discipline, truth, and devotion to personal development can be of benefit to all. Everything is connected, and we create our life through self-mastery.

Begin by structuring your day and applying the tips and tools at the end of each chapter for a more spiritual mindset and experience. In this way, you can bring joy into your life and eventually you will discover your multidimensional nature. I hope this information assists you on your journey to becoming powerful Beings.

As you navigate your way through this book, look at the fruit you have gained. Is it about helping you elevate and empower yourself, love, be joyful, learn about yourself, heal, release the past, and be of service – or not? This is the litmus test and only you can know if it helps you. As always, this book reflects my understanding on my journey at this time.

Blessings and enjoy!

Pete

Chapter 1
UPON AWAKENING

How you start your day sets the stage for what follows. If done in a productive manner, it can be joyful and productive, and over time it will become second nature. So create a morning ritual/routine that supports having a blissful, fruitful day and overall existence.

Being productive, healthy, and happy comes back to acknowledging the good things and having gratitude and thanking that which created all: Source. We are always connected to Source, the intelligence we are all a part of, come from, and go back to.

Source, God, Creator, Great Spirit, call it what you like, goes by many names. This intelligence is all loving, always there, and it hears our every thought and word. It is non-judgmental and, like a parent, it is always there for us, its children.

As I followed the path of self-inquiry and healing, and adapted to multidimensional mind and self-mastery, I naturally started to talk with God. I spent time with God. This might seem strange to some, but anyone can do it at any time. When you make it your intention, God is just a thought away.

Happy, successful people usually live in a spiritual way. For some, it comes naturally. Others come to learn it because something inside of them leads them. The fact is that we are all one consciousness and the reality we experience is a projection from within.

Of course, we all have what we perceive to be challenges. We can choose to see these challenges as opportunities, an adventure for growth that leads to more and more opportunities, experiences, wisdom, and knowledge during our evolutionary process.

Determination, enthusiasm, and inspiration are essential tools for living a fruitful life, but coming from a place of joy is key. Anger, bitterness, obsessiveness, jealousy, and ego can be bitter for the soul and spirit. Of course, negativity can affect those around you and your happiness, mental health, and well-being. Everyone has their own way of doing things, their own triggers and mechanics of the mind. This is something all of us must find out for ourselves.

There are different aspects of the mind, body, and spirit (energetic aspect), and unless all of these aspects are recognized, nourished, and exercised, an unbalanced life can unfold. Thus, we need to nurture our physical and non-physical aspects.

With this said, I am not going to tell you to go and sit on top of a mountain and meditate for hours on end every day, not unless you want to. But try to embrace the meditative state, a joyful state during the day when working or playing. This experience is available for all and it is very beneficial for a purposeful and happy life.

One of the many ways to unfold a joyful state is by connecting within to the Source of all things, God, and acknowledging and working with it. This universal intelligence is everywhere. You are a cell of Source, and when you acknowledge this, give thanks and reconnect with it, you will start to see your path, your journey, and most of all you will live in a blissful state. This state can assist you in living with purpose and passion, which includes being of service to others.

To connect to Source is not hard; you are already connected to it and to the mind behind the mind. The state in which you witness yourself observing this reality is the place in which you are aware and know you are aware. This state is shapeless, formless, and unbounded. It is your true nature, which is all-knowing and pure love.

Acknowledging this intelligence and tuning into it starts to build a stronger connection, a cohesive relationship, as the recognition on your part becomes stronger each time you acknowledge and work with it. You become more symbiotic with The Creator and your energetic nature.

Connecting to Source as a part of your morning routine is all it takes to strengthen and exercise the connection. Much can change very quickly; intention is all it takes and coming from the heart.

Establishing a conscious connection to Source when starting out on the path to self-mastery can be healing, because it is a path of rediscovering your true nature. Realizing the past and all that doesn't serve you will bring in new energies and create a joyful life. Some do it kicking and screaming and make it more complicated than it needs to be. They swim upstream, so to speak, rather than going with the flow. Change is a given and you can either embrace it – or not. The choice is up to you.

Self Mastery – The Path to Ascension

Many people think Masters and gurus can solve all their problems. They think they can follow and devote themselves to these Beings and everything will be fixed. However, a true Master helps us find our own way using tips and tools. They do not fix everything for us.

Some people have certain expectations. They think going outside of themselves will bring enlightenment and self-realization. This might seem easy, but it has many shortcomings. The Master is within. There is no shortcut. We each have our own path to reconnect to the Master. Let it unfold easily and naturally. You are unique and this makes you a rare jewel and an asset to not just those around you, but to the universe as a whole.

Fractal in nature, we are connected through the blueprint of an intelligence forgotten by most until the time comes to reunite with it. Source! Self-mastery is about carrying this connection with you all day every day, no matter what arises.

Before you are enlightened, you wake up, have a shower, brush your teeth, and then go about your day. *After* you are enlightened, you wake up, have a shower, brush your teeth, and go about your day.

Self Mastery – The Path to Ascension

The only time it is not like this is when you shed your physical form and reconnect with your garment of light, your Light Body. So, get used to this experience, unless it is your path in this life to ascend to the level of Light Body status. Either way, we all go back to what we came from. We become Creator Beings in the most in-depth way, although if you can already see your true potential, you are a Creator Being in physical form right now.

From the present moment forward you can make the changes that are needed. Like a seed, watch the plant of change grow and mould the reality you want. It all depends on how you view this reality.

Change starts with the intention to connect with Source and, most of all, allow it to work through you. You can be a vehicle for Source to work through. For some, this might be uncomfortable, but by getting out of the way and letting God work through you, much can change and be achieved in a multiplicity of ways.

All this comes down to spending time with God first thing every day. Whether you pray or simply talk to God, go about it in your own way and do what feels right. You might be surprised by the changes that occur in your energy, your life, and your surroundings.

Spending time with God doesn't cost a thing and it can be done anywhere, anytime. All it needs is to be nurtured and watered a little every day. You just need to make time for your relationship with God/Source. A minute at the very least each day can be enough. The more you connect with God/Source, the more it will work through you. Now how hard can that be?

Exercises – Tips and Tools

Check-In and Tune In

When you wake up in the morning, first observe your thoughts, feelings, and emotions. This needs to be done on a regular basis. Clearings can assist, and I will go into them later, plus many other simple and practical exercises.

From this place, witness your thoughts, ideas, and feelings; don't be attached. They are not you, so don't identify with them. This is done for a reason that will soon make sense.

Connect to Source

Try starting your day by creating your own ritual to connect to Source/God. If you have a sacred space, use this spot, because each time you do your practices, you're creating a portal, a vortex that builds the positive energy, thins the veils between worlds more and more, and uplifts the energies that will amplify and create a sacred, high vibrational space. Now set the intention to connect to Source.

You could burn incense, although this isn't a must. Then visualize a ball of light in your heart space area, whatever color you intuitively feel it to be. And then, with intention, visualize it expanding until your whole body and even your environment is engulfed in this light (use your imagination, if need be, as imagination is creation). Next repeat your prayer to God, Source, whatever you like to call the consciousness that we are all a part of.

In your own way, and if you want to, give thanks for your heartbeat, every breath, the people in your life, your partner, parents, children, family, friends, etc. (Name them if you want to.) Give thanks and gratitude for your food, shelter, clothing, health, and if open to it, tell God that you are a vehicle for Source to work through. Tell God that you accept the blessings and abundance that comes with being a vehicle. Ask for assistance tapping into and using the knowledge and wisdom within to make the right decisions and be of service, as well as assist with being happy. Ask for clarity and balance in your mind, body, and spirit connection. You can also send healing and supportive energies to those you know who might need it and the world, even yourself. Just talk with God! Do it from the heart.

Check-In and Tune in Again

Now, take a moment and check your feelings. Do you feel different than before you connected to Source? If you woke up on the wrong side of the bed or your energies felt low, this should be rectified now.

Chapter 2
ASSESS AND CLEAR

Every day is an opportunity to experience what The Creator has to offer and for you to create, too, as you are also a Creator Being. We are only limited by our imagination, and Imagination is creation. Every moment we are one step closer to our transition back to the other side and what you make of each moment is your decision.

You will eventually be judged by the fruit of your actions, and you are also the judge. Every moment there is a new experience, an opportunity, a joyful experience to be had if you are open to it and focused in the present.

Too often, when waking up in the morning, some people are worried about what they have to do that day or what isn't working in their life. They are not thinking about how beautiful it is to wake up to another day or the wonderment of "What am I going to do today?"

Chores always need doing; that's just the way it is. Responsibilities are part of physical existence and this is a given, but how we react and our perception of this reality is up to us. As the old saying goes, "You can see things as a cup half empty or half full." Setting the stage for the day via a positive mindset can transform your existence into a new plateau. Spending time with God, The Creator, Source, whatever you like to call it, can help set the energy in a positive way. This can be done by just focusing on the present moment.

This is very simple and anyone can do it. For some, it might be meditation, but labels don't matter. Simply setting your intention to just be will take you far on the path of self-awareness. The problems of the world will dissolve as you decide how and where to place your awareness, attention, and energy.

The mechanics of the mind can easily be affected and unproductive if you don't know yourself first. To know yourself is to know God.

You are not your thoughts and your possessions. You are an unbounded being with a pinpoint of your God Self Awareness having a human experience. This is one of the realizations recognized on the path to self-mastery.

Self Mastery – The Path to Ascension

Although there are exceptions, you will find some are in a joyful and present state embracing life without limit. This way is just natural for them.

Some look at this behavior and say ignorance is bliss, maybe. But in some cases, as I have stated before, if you or those you love would give the shirt off their back to a fellow human being, then they're a good person. They are doing their walk here by just being a good person; they don't need this spiritual information because they are simply good people. These are the basics of Ascension and a joyful life. It is that simple. What we need in the world currently is for people to be loving, caring, and of assistance to others. Being joyful brings joy to all.

In terms of taking it to the next level when on the path of self-mastery (which Ascension is a by-product of) discipline is key, no matter your age, location, advantages or disadvantages. To grow, evolve, learn, and be successful (and I am not talking about financially or possession-wise) discipline is essential for self-mastery. Gaining knowledge and having a positive mindset, outlook, manifesting capabilities, drive, health and well-being, discipline and enjoying the journey is a must, whether things are going your way or not.

Epigenetics, upbringing, education, and social engineering cause us to face some form of trials and tribulations. The poor go without, the rich chase happiness, and everyone has their view, outlook, desires, and values. People are always chasing the next thing and, in most cases, thinking the next thing they are chasing will bring them happiness. This is not the case. Just being happy in the present moment throughout each step of your journey is something most of us need to master in the human experience.

Chasing enlightenment, wanting to be a Master or guru, and desiring contact with otherworldly Beings is a distraction, but it is also accessible. These experiences come with the journey when we master our own thoughts and actions. All of us have experienced something we can't explain. We are in a simulation. We are cells of the same body working in unison. Herein lies the fundamental basis of how this reality works. What you say and do affects everyone and everything. But it goes a little deeper, too. It isn't only what you say, but what you think.

There are many negative influences in the world that affect humanity, including certain people, media, organizations, secret societies, thought forms, and entities that masquerade and parade within. Connecting to the God within can disable these energies. But with that said, the biggest influence that can hold us back from our own evolutionary process is ourselves.

Mastery of the mind is of key importance. Your environment also has an effect in setting the stage for your day. It can be joyful and exciting, or it can be the opposite. How you eat and exercise, who you surround yourself with, where you live, and what you do have an impact on your existence.

Assessing where you can make changes in your evolutionary process, which is ongoing as you refine yourself, is constant and ongoing. And remember, Source/The Creator, is doing the same through us.

Even after Gautama Buddha became enlightened, he still had to eat and deal with what most see as mundane, although when you are enlightened you can do everything with joy, with ease, and with flow. Things are only as hard as you make them out to be. It's your energy that decides.

Negative, positive, happy, sad – all emotions are to be experienced. Be the flow of energy of what feels good, what feels right. This can make life easy. Use this as your gauge, "Does what I am doing feel right? Does what I am doing bring me bliss? Do my actions affect others, and if so, how?"

Why is it that ninety percent of the news, movies, and gossip is negative, sad, and upsetting? Because we as a civilization have been programmed to see negativity as exciting and entertaining. There's a rush that comes with it. This influence has been solely taught and programmed into the Earth human from negative influences, affecting individuals and (in effect) the collective's mindset. However, all can be reprogrammed. This is not just a local thing to the Earth and its inhabitants, either, but rather far-reaching to other worlds and realms.

One thing I would say is that most people just want to be happy. For this, discipline and changes need to be made in order to see what isn't working, followed by trying new things and learning to come from the heart when making choices. Just sitting for a moment with The Creator/Source first thing in the morning can go a long way.

Dissolve into nothingness, which is everything. Sometimes thoughts and ideas will come through. What is the fruit of these thoughts? This is how we can gauge whether the information is beneficial or not.

Dissolving whatever is not in alignment with us can take time and require the cutting of cords. The cord-cutting process I'm referring to is not just a Tibetan practice. Many other cultures have been doing it for a long time, as well as off-world in the Pleiades Star Cluster and the Orion Constellation.

Some people don't know what they want and that's fine. But one thing everyone does know is what they *don't* want. On the path of self-mastery, cutting cords, releasing the past, and moving forwards is a must. For this, discipline is needed. No one can make the changes you want except you. Cutting cords can assist with releasing relationships, soul contracts (which can be changed at any time), and undesirable entities. There are many applications and doing it from the heart is key. Staying within the Guidelines of Universal Law is a must. The heart is the guidance system as to what is and what isn't within these guidelines.

The heart is a marvelous biological device. It gives off a bigger magnetic field than the brain and it affects those around us and our environment. It also taps into the Light Body, forming a connection straight to Source.

Clearing negative influences, entities, attachments, parasitic thought forms, ethereal implants, and our own guilt, traumas, and judgment assists with healing and being rooted in our own authority and power. Doing Clearings is of great importance.

A Clearing is a type of prayer. With intention, it works on multiple levels. When saying it, feeling it, putting your intention on it, and even visualizing, you are in a ball of light in the introductory phases. This is how you can start to work and operate multidimensionally. (See Tips and Tools at the end of this chapter for instructions on doing a Clearing.)

Any unseen influences from spirits that have passed beyond the physical and are in a lower vibrational state, lower light intelligences that have a self-serving agenda, and even negative thoughts about you from others – there are many ways we can be affected, but there are ways to clear these influences. This is what a Clearing does.

It is best to do a Clearing every day at the time best suited for you, more often if needed. I do Clearings myself at least three times a day. Discipline assists with this becoming second nature, to the point that Clearings can be done in a second by just thinking about it. Even with negative thoughts coming from elsewhere, recognition of the thought not being yours and saying "this is not mine" can stop and neutralize this negativity because you have acknowledged it and brought it out into the open.

Many years ago, I was known for assisting people in their homes and other locations with hauntings, house clearings, and entity removals. I still do this from time to time, but as my own personal experiences continued there was a backlash. Disturbing entities tried to divert me off my path. (More information on this can be found in my books *Awakening: UFOs and Other Strange Happenings* and *Operation Starseed: A Temporal War*.)

But then I was visited by the helpful Positive Elohim, Shi-Ji, and the Guardians. Shi-Ji was of assistance, and later I found out she is another aspect of myself from the Pleiades. Talk about mind-bending!

As an introduction to the Positive Elohim, the main ones are a light electric blue liquid light, but there are different colors spanning the rainbow. Some stay in the blueprint of Source, while others are doing things here and there as Creator Beings within God's mind. Some look like they are on fire and they can go from being an orb to manifesting as whatever they like, such as a column of light or liquid light seven-foot-tall humanoid beings that are neither male nor female.

There is also the service to others carried out by the Positive Elohim, who work in synch with Metatron, Michael, and the Angelic collective, the Guardians, the Watchers, and the Ascended Masters. There are ETs including the Lyrans, Orions, Pleiadians, Sirians, Arcturians, Andromedans from the Constellation and the Andromedan Galaxy, the nature and inner Earth beings, and ultra-terrestrials, local and afar, just to mention a few and what's local to us.

Then there are the Fallen Elohim who have lost a lot of their capabilities and are not at the level of enlightenment and transdimensional capabilities. They are responsible for the creation of Artificial Intelligence and its ability to feed off negative energy and hold a frequency so they can stay outside of Source. Let's just say service to self got a hold of them through their egos.

The negative, I came to find out, serves the purpose of letting us recognize what we don't want to experience. Therefore, if we can raise our frequency, we will be above the lower vibration and, thus, ascend beyond the negative vibration. It's a Catch-22 scenario.

I call these negative intelligences collectively the *Lower Light*, as they are void of Light. They are also known as *The Archon Network*, which has at its leadership the fallen ones of the Elohim. And I am not talking about the Biblical version! That's a replay of what's in other worlds and what has happened in other dimensions, and then replicated itself throughout cycles in this galaxy and beyond.

Any negativity we encounter in our spiritual evolution is a test to eventually reunite us with our higher selves and become Creator Beings capable of creating our own universes. We each become a universe unto ourselves, a cell of a greater intelligence.

In a short period of time, some visitors shed light on my situation. Yeshua (Jesus) appeared! I was struck by his complete love and compassion when he appeared physically in my home for a short period of time with the telepathic message that I must fight these battles when I am attacked, and that He and others would be there for guidance, but that ultimately it is up to me. Yeshua said that throughout this period, I would learn what I am capable of. You could say I was in an extreme and high level of boot camp. Looking back, I now see this as a high level of on-the-job training for what I am doing now. I needed to experience the extreme dark in order to help others find their own light within.

Around this time, I became reacquainted with an old friend from another existence, a feline being called *Patma* from the Sirius Star System.

I was in a bad way when three of these Beings appeared. They seemed familiar. I was on my lazy boy couch with my eyes closed, and in my Mind's Eye (*Third Eye*) I could see where I was in real-time physically when they came in. But when I opened my eyes, I saw an apparition form of them physically but very faintly. Patma was one of these Beings and our contacts have continued for many years.

The reason for this visit was to assist me with a healing and also reacquaint me with how I can do healing myself. My energy bands looked like a rainbow being pulled out and tuned like an instrument as the three Beings manipulated the bands with intuition and Source guidance. They recalibrated the bands to be where they should be. Experiencing this and the accompanying informational downloads re-awakened within me the Sirian form of healing and other techniques the

Pleiadians and Arcturians use. Now I use whatever is necessary.

Most of us have all been in other worlds, so these visitors were old friends. Some of this recall arises from an experience I had when energy hit me while meditating and I flipped off my couch into my gas heater and heard a voice say, "More of you." A short time after this experience, visions of other lives came to me. It was a lot to integrate.

Another intelligence that assisted me during this period is a Master Being from Orion called *Penkay*. Through physical visits, including communication via thought transfer, visions, and downloads, I remembered a peaceful warrior side of him. During this time, I was unraveling my own guidance within to find my path, and this got me through this period because I saw what all of us are capable of.

Penkay and I still connect on the odd occasion, and when I have interactions with the Elohim, Penkay might teleport in, come at me in his Light Body, and we teleport to meeting places in other worlds or realms. Sometimes, I just find myself in these places and my greater family comes to see me.

With all this said, no intelligences are to be looked up to, but to be seen as family or a conduit for a lesson we need to learn. Just look at the fruit gained from your experiences. I also know we have everything we need within us, although sometimes it must be pointed out in order to be recognized, especially when attacks are coming and we are in the thick of it.

At times, we need patience. We need to be open to another point of view, but also enjoy the journey. Too many people want to be more spiritual, but they don't understand a lot of what is going on.

Here are a couple of charts describing intelligences of a positive and negative nature and the dimensional aspect of their existence. I collaborated with James Gilliland in creating these charts. By no means do they cover every being and all the possible information. They are just a frame of reference.

Also included is a chart on densities, as there is a difference between this and other dimensions. The way I can explain it at this time is that densities represent the level of consciousness determining which dimensional realms we can access and experience.

An extra chart is presented to show how in science today we can only measure and experience such a small aspect of the universe. In this case, the electromagnetic spectrum, and the visible light spectrum we can see is just a slither of that.

Beings operate throughout the electromagnetic spectrum in infrared and UV. Cameras show this, at times. For example, I have been able to film my experiences of an otherworldly nature using an infrared camera.

INTELLIGENCES WITHIN SOURCE

10-13D & Beyond	Ascended Collective – The Elohim – The Angelic Kingdom
9D	Lyran Godman and Goddess Beings
8D	Andromeda Galaxy Beings
7D	Arcturians – Pleiadians – Sirians – Lyrans – Orions – Lion Beings – Anunnaki
6D	Pleiadians – Sirian Panther Beings – Orion Council of Light – Inner Earth Beings
5D	Pleiadians – Sirian Felines – Orions – Andromeda Constellation Beings – Alpha Centaurians – Ascended Masters – Inner Earth Beings
4D	Some Ascended Masters – Inner Earth Beings – Neutral Greys – The Watchers
3D	Humanity

जया

NEGATIVE INTELLIGENCES WITHIN SOURCE

- The Fallen Elohim – Fallen Angels – Demonic Entities – Shadow Beings
- Artificial Intelligence
- Archons – Serpent Beings – Some Tall Greys – The Fallen Anunnaki
- Royal and Draco Reptilians – Reptilian Greys – Some Small Greys
- Thought Forms – Wounded Intelligences – Discarnate Souls – Trickster

Lower 4D

जया

Self Mastery – The Path to Ascension

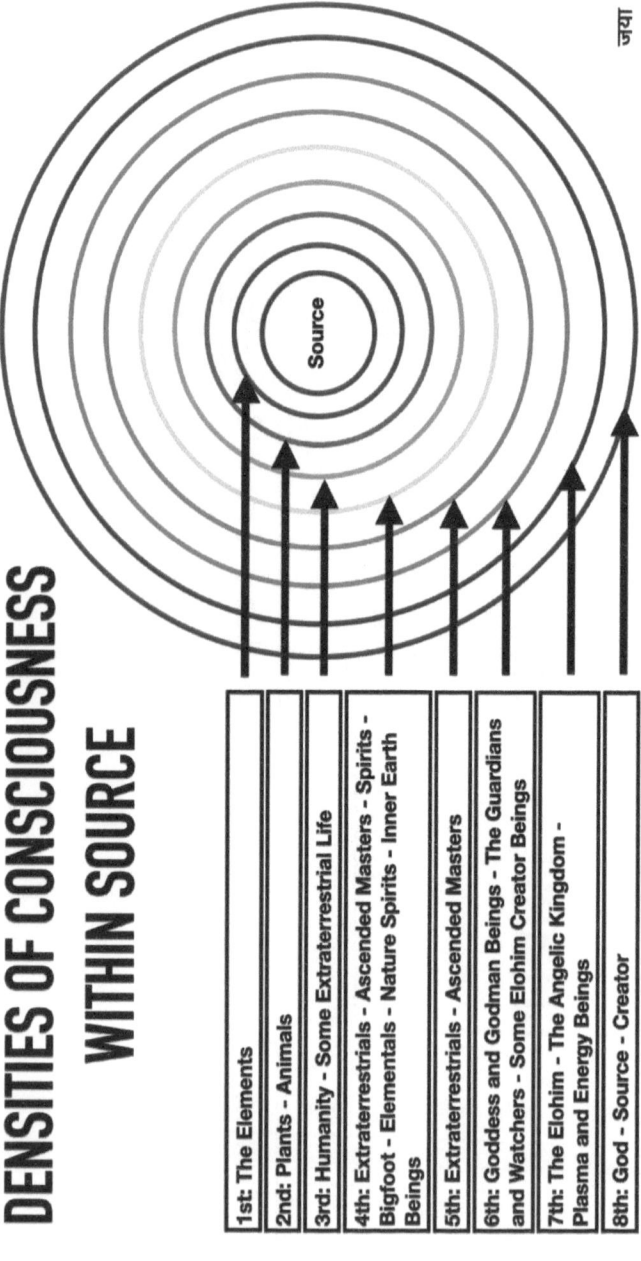

CONSCIOUSNESS EXPRESSED THROUGH THE ELECTROMAGNETIC SPECTRUM

- Hertzian
- Infrared
- Visible Light
- Ultraviolet
- X-Ray
- Gamma Ray

We can only see a fraction of 0.005% of the electromagnetic spectrum which is visible light

Self Mastery – The Path to Ascension

Many influences affect us energetically and physically. Diseases and the like can manifest and/or mental illnesses, anxiety, frustration and lower energy levels. Love and forgiveness for ourselves is key in this process, but God/Source needs to be placed first. For some, and rightly so, evidence of this can seal the deal and show us how big and beautiful this reality is.

Evidence for one person is not evidence for another, but rather a by-product that comes when we are going through an awakening/transformation. Ask and you shall receive. From there, just take notice of whatever unfolds that might seem synchronistic; there's no such thing as a coincidence. During this process, the beautiful Masters, Angels, ETs and their crafts might even make an appearance, whether you are in the waking or dream state.

There is family beyond this world, behind the veil from which you have come, and there is much you have already explored that is part of your experience here. Now begins your journey to explore being human. You have walked many worlds, done many things, and it comes down to experience and gleaning knowledge. Enjoy the journey!

This world just needs a little work and that work first needs to be done within. From this, great changes will come about for the collective if enough of us participate.

Like the Maharishi Effect, when crime was lowered via meditation, your thoughts, intention, and energy not only affect your environment or what you surround yourself with, but ultimately the collective. For great changes in the world, we must first make great changes in ourselves.

Spending time with God, even if you start out for just a moment every day, can bring about an amazing transformation. Let the Flame of Source purify you.

With that said, the flame of fire is an amazing element that can assist in burning up that which no longer serves you. It can also increase your enthusiasm, determination, and inspiration. Be like fire, be like the Flame, be like Source.

Exercises – Tips and Tools

Be With God

Even if it's for a minute or two, just be with God. Know that if your eyes are closed or open, all is a part of The Creator and if you are in tune with The Creator, you can start to manifest and direct your life in a beneficial direction, although you might not see it that way at the time. The more you work with just being present (which is being in The Creator's presence) when making decisions, guidance is just a thought away. In the present, observe/witness your breath and simply sit. Take notice of any thoughts and ideas that come through, because this can be directly from The Creator.

Check-In

Tune into how you are feeling and the difference in your feeling and energies compared to when waking up and keep the positive flow going. At this point, if you still feel a bit stagnant, and even if you don't, try doing a Clearing.

This is a must to start your day, and I recommend doing it again at lunch, dinner and even before bed.

Introduction to Clearings

A Clearing is a type of prayer. Having the intention to clear your space, feeling your intention, stating your intention, and visualizing it adds levels to the Clearing and amplifies the effects.

Doing a Clearing can shift and uplift your energies. Sometimes, negative influences, thought-forms, past spirits, negative and trickster entities, negative extraterrestrials, and even just our own thoughts can put us into a lower state of consciousness and energy. People we know (or don't know), or ill thoughts from others about us, can cause us to have low energies and negative thoughts. Sometimes, ethereal cords from past or present relationships can bring us into a lower vibrational state, so this is why Clearings are important. Clearings have a positive and uplifting effect by neutralizing the influences from negative energies.

The Clearing techniques that follow are not the only way for Clearings to be done. Make up your own method and do what works for you. This is just a brief outline of the techniques I teach and sometimes use myself. Remember, imagination is creation. Also, you might want to use the check-in technique before and after each practice as a way to gauge if and how effective each practice is for you.

Clearing Technique 1

Start by imagining yourself engulfed in white, golden, violet, or blue-colored light; use whatever colored light you prefer. Then say words that work for you, silently or out loud. Here are examples of the words I use:

1. I ask those who are aligned with the healing of the Earth and the awakening of humanity to connect to my consciousness.

2. I ask the native spirits in my area and Gaia (Mother Earth) to connect to my consciousness. I also ask for their blessing to be here.

3. I ask the nature spirits and elementals in alignment with me to connect with my consciousness.

4. I now ask my Guides, the Masters, Saints, Sages, the Beings I work with, and my own God Self to connect with my consciousness.

5. I also ask that any psychic bonds and connections that are not positive be dissolved, along with any negative implants and attachments.

6. I ask the healing energies to step forward and assist with any physical, mental, or emotional healing I might need.

7. Let anything that is not in alignment with me be escorted by their Guides to where they need to go. Let them know they can change the state they're in, and let them know they are loved, healed, and forgiven.

8. Finally, blast yourself again with whatever colored light you choose.

Clearing Technique 2

Visualize yourself breathing in a color or feeling that is therapeutic, loving, and revitalizing for you. As you breathe out, relax the muscles in your face around your eyes, cheeks, jaw, and neck. Breathe the loving energy in again, and breathe out any tension in your shoulders, back, arms, and stomach. Breathe in the loving energy again and breathe out any tension from your hips down to your toes; then continue breathing the loving energy in and out.

Next go into the Clearing, stating: "I call upon my Guides, Higher Self, and God/Source/Creator." Follow this with:

"I ask that any cords, attachments, implants, parasitic thought forms, anything not aligned with the awakening and healing of humanity and the Earth and my mission and journey be dissolved or escorted to its perfect place. Go in peace."

Self Mastery – The Path to Ascension

You might want to imagine that you are engulfed in light at this point.

Next, state: "I now ask the healing energies to step forward and go throughout the molecular structure of my body, organs, emotional body, and Light Body as a whole, balancing out, rectifying, and enhancing energies where needed for my optimal efficiency."

"I ask for a blessing from Gaia, the original spirits of the land, nature spirits, elementals, plant and animal spirits, as well as inner Earth and the celestial and star family. I also pray for a blessing from God/Source/Creator."

"I ask to be sealed off in a dome of protection, immune from any outside influences, and that only my main teacher and Spirit Guides, Higher Self, and Source can step into this dome to assist with guidance, direction, service to others, abundance, peace, love, and joy, and balance of mind, body and spirit, as well as passion and purpose. Thank you."

The following is an example of a short Clearing prayer referring to the Lords of Light, an Elohim intelligence:

Pete's Unbounded Prayer

"I call upon the Lords of Light to take all beings to the light. Let them know they are healed and free. Blessed they are. So may it be."

Cutting Cords

This practice can be used at any time for healing, releasing traumas, judgment, relationships, forgiveness, and the past.

Call upon your Higher Self, Source, a Master, Spirit Guide, or even Kwan Yin, the Goddess of Compassion and Protector of Children, who is great and effective in assisting in the cutting cord process.

From this point, visualize the person, event, or whatever else you might want to release, and visualize a cord made of light connecting you to it. If visualization doesn't work so well for you, focus on sensing it.

From this place, send love, forgiveness, and thanks to whatever you are releasing. Imagine your arm is a sword of light and bring it down from above in front of your head, and continue down across just in front of your heart and down to your waist area, as you cut the cord attaching you to the event or person you want to detach from.

I recommend doing this at least three times or until you feel a release.

From this point, put your hands over the area where you feel the cord was cut and send yourself love for as long as you feel you need to.

This process can sometimes take multiple attempts and might need to be done over a few days, depending on the depth of whatever you are releasing.

Remember, imagination is creation. You might cry, you might get emotional, but remember, your tears are releasing the toxins in your system and this is also part of the healing process.

Ignite the Flame

This is another exercise that can help with protection and assist you in connecting with the love of Source and your Godself. First, visualize with your imagination a ball of light over your heart. Another way of doing this is to simply sense the energy.

Self Mastery – The Path to Ascension

Visualize with intention a ball of light the size of a golf ball in any color over your heart. See it or feel it spinning and flickering, and then slowly through intention or feeling, expand it slowly until your whole body is engulfed in this energy. Take your time and, remember, it's all about intention.

Now, expand the energy like an explosion going out and around your environment, and then suck it back around your body and see or feel it spinning and swirling around you. You might feel static energy around you or on your skin, a bit like goose bumps. There might be temperature changes, a shift in your energy and feelings of clearness and a balance of energy. At this time, and even when meditating in general, you might start to rock back and forth. This can be caused by the Light Body and energy body affecting the physical body. It's a kind of by-product, so don't worry. Just go with the flow and keep on rocking.

To understand the effects and changes of this exercise, emotionally and physically, you might want to use the Check-in Technique to see how this practice works for you.

House Clearing

This is very simple, although how much you put into it is what will come from it. A simple way to go about this is to move all the furniture you can or rearrange it, whatever feels right. Then lightly sprinkle salt around the house, not too much. Next, put on some positive, uplifting music, the more bass and drums the better. Then leave the house anywhere from thirty minutes to several hours, if you can without upsetting your neighbors.

The vibration of the music, with assistance from the salt and moving the furniture, will break up, neutralize, and uplift the light blueprint in your home.

Just like us, our environment can become stagnant or depressed and we need to let in the light with a house clearing. Doing this every few months can help create a positive vibe in the home or office and uplift the energies for happiness, productivity, and relaxation.

Using Sage

Sage was used by the ancient people in America and up until modern times. It is said that burning sage (also called *smudging*) can help clear the environment.

I like to break off a quarter of a stick of sage, lightly crumble it down into a clay bowl, and light it. Then I do a Clearing as I walk into each room and move the bowl in a circular motion three times clockwise and sometimes counter-clockwise. It all depends on what you intuitively feel in the center of each space and/or room. Sometimes, I also walk around my out-buildings and inside them if they have been occupied or I feel they need it. Sometimes, I repeat a mantra evoking love, light, and bliss as I visualize the smoke being filled with the energy of these words. In this way, I can clear the whole environment.

If I'm only clearing the house, I let whatever is left in the bowl burn out on the deck by the front door.

Creating a Crystal Grid

A crystal grid provides an extra layer of protection for your space and home. There are many ways you can go about this, but the easiest is to get five quartz crystals and cleanse and clear them by putting them under running water or leaving them in a stream and then in the sun.

You can do this for an hour, a day, or more often; use your intuition when cleansing them. Then do a Clearing with the crystals. Finally, program them through thought with the intention of protecting the home through the grid you are going to make connecting them to each other.

To create your grid, put one cleansed crystal in each corner of the property and (as best you can) put one in the middle of it. They can be buried slightly or sit somewhere safe.

As you are putting each crystal in its place, visualize a beam of light going to the next one you are going to put in place. With the middle one, visualize a beam going up above and down below the property, and that all the others connect to this beam. After all five are in place, you will have created a pyramid of protection … not just above in a square pyramid, but above and below in an octahedron.

Make sure to check the grid on a regular basis through intuition, and send it love and light when needed to keep it powered up. If necessary, also cleanse the crystals periodically.

Chapter 3
HEART AND MIND COHERENCE

Are you living the life you want? Due to outside circumstances, some of us are not. This is not to be negative, but to point out the obvious. For a great change, great changes you must make.

Knowing and feeling what you are putting out to manifest is a key to transforming your life and creating the reality you want. "Desire" and "want" are not the words that should be used here, but I am using them to make this material digestible. "I have, I am" should be used instead. Do you feel the difference? Affirmations are of value, and they are free and can be done anytime. Affirmations can transform your trajectory.

I got talking once with a millionaire years ago about abundance. He said that he gets up at 5:00 a.m. every day to do power walking. And while walking he repeats affirmations. He also said that as soon as money starts coming in, he tries to figure out how to give it away. Talk about creating your reality and being of service to others.

Sometimes, a detour in our direction occurs. At first, the detour might seem like it is taking us away from something or someone, or in a different direction than what we are in the process of manifesting. However, a detour might be bringing us closer to our objectives than we realize.

For example, let's pretend your goal is to go to the supermarket (nothing lavish or hard to manifest). You get in the car, follow your normal route, and then you come across road work and there is a detour sign in the middle of the road blocking your normal way to the supermarket. So you make the turn and find yourself driving a way you might have never driven before, and soon you're at the supermarket.

What I am saying here is that sometimes when the unexpected happens, a change in plans occurs. The unexpected brings opportunity; in this case, not only to get to the place you desired to go, but also your plans might come to fruition quicker. In addition, you might have avoided an accident that could have happened further along your original route. When things don't go according to plan, try to be positive and optimistic, and remain in a blissful and exuberant state. Putting out and feeling what you are putting out for is key. But then there is also meeting the universe halfway and creating opportunities.

The flip side is that sometimes you need to drop the how, the wondering, the stress of it all and your obsessiveness, and simply let the universe bring everything to you. Of course, this is on a case-by-case basis, and you need to follow your heart through feeling and assessing each situation. Given that all is one consciousness, when you are in the midst of a transformation, manifesting and following your heart is key. The inner and outer mechanics of the universe can unfold in unimaginable ways.

Gratitude through prayer and thanking others is a must and should not need to be pointed out. But due to the lower vibrational state many are in nowadays and current circumstances in the world, this reminder to be grateful does need to be pointed out. Expressing gratitude should also be a part of your routine of daily practices and mindset. Affirmations are just the icing on the cake; the most rewarding and joyful things are free.

A hug, love, a touch, and being in nature with family and friends, a conversation – these things money can't buy. The heart is activated by experiences like these, which are natural and free.

Feeling gratitude from the heart and having the attitude of gratitude can transform your energy, your environment, and your circumstances. For some, it doesn't happen overnight, but know this: anything is possible. I am a witness and an example of this, and so are many others around the world.

The victim mentality can only take you so far, but forgiveness for yourself and others and having compassion and drive to succeed can be of assistance. You need to make changes and alter your path. Discipline is also needed to keep on the path of Ascension and your evolutionary process.

Just like the story of the tortoise and the hare, don't judge a book by its cover. Your own perception can be your demise, if you are in judgment and not operating from the heart space. At first, something might seem impossible, but the impossible is always possible.

Determination, outlook, and creative thinking from the heart can bring about change and opportunities in an instant, but what you do with this is up to you. Don't let anyone tell you what you can or cannot achieve. Only you can limit your opportunities and progress.

The Field

Feelings from the heart tap into the field, the Light Body, as above, so below. Let me put this into perspective.

Some yogis call this field *energy* or *Shakti*. Others call it *prana* or *chi*, and some call this field *God*. Others might call it the *quantum field*, *ether*, or *zero point*. There are many other names. The point is that everything is connected and comes from and goes back to this field. There is the mind and the body, and then there is this field, or energy. All is connected and comes from it. Everything is just a different manifestation and state of it. Like Albert Einstein said, E=Mc2.

Everything is in a different state or form of this energy – and energy doesn't dissolve. It just transforms from one state to another, and it cannot be destroyed. Tapping into this field from the heart, whether for gratitude or manifesting, is important.

This is where prayer, affirmations, attitude and way of life come into play in order to make the most joyful life a reality. Something as simple as a couple of minutes of prayer and affirmations can go a long way in bringing that which you are putting out for into physical manifestation. And once you get the ball rolling, it can transform your life, which means you now have an opportunity to assist others with transforming their lives in ways that will be revealed through intuition and inner guidance.

None of what is being mentioned here is new. We are all guides and teachers to each other, although how we express our experiences is different. Like snowflakes, we are all unique.

We are all children of The Creator and we are learning to become creators ourselves. Earth is the school of all schools, and operations are in play to help transform the Earth human society from within.

Many are shocked by the outside world because of the wars and injustices. However, what we do to ourselves individually can be far worse and inflict more suffering than any war or trauma from an external source.

To heal, we must forgive and be open to new experiences. We must be open to opportunities and embrace not just the unexpected but expect to be uncomfortable. Ride the energy with excitement, wonderment, and be childlike. Embrace all of your experiences and the wonder this world has to offer, as it builds and builds and has a snowball effect in which all is amplified in the field of positive energy. In this place, you will be predominately in an optimistic, happy, cup half-full state, rather than always seeing the downside in a situation. Unfortunately, too many operate in this way currently.

The Age of Enlightenment is upon us, and if you can take it and accept it, the moment of enlightenment will be instantaneous. You are in control. What you decide is up to you, but again it comes back to the fact that for great change, you must make great choices. Some would say sacrifices, but if you see it as a sacrifice to dissolve the negative in order to embrace something new and positive, this is not an issue. It's progress.

All anyone wants is to be happy, to smile, laugh, and see their loved ones and their fellow humans do the same. If all of us take a moment to set the intention for our lives to be enjoyed, not as a chore but to make it our nature, transformation is just an action away, a thought away. Nothing is out of reach; if you can imagine it, you can manifest it. This is so simple. The mind is connected to the Spirit, the Holy Spirit, and from there we create through thought. As above, so below – all is only a thought away.

Also, don't forget to smile. It takes little energy to smile. When you do, your smile emanates out into the world, affecting your field and others in your environment. Your smile uplifts the whole world.

Self Mastery – The Path to Ascension

Exercises – Tips and Tools

Affirmations

Affirming something means stating out loud with feeling what you want to bring into your life, thereby drawing it into the now and into a process of manifesting through positive thinking, feeling, and being. In this way, you are affirming your intention, which connects to consciousness and allows you to tap into the physical light blueprint of this reality where all is first manifest.

Affirmations can be very productive; they can assist with reprogramming your upbringing, education, social engineering, or Epigenetics, all that has had an unproductive effect on you. Affirmations can help you release the past in order to heal and manifest a positive present.

It's not just repeating the affirmations that's important, but the choice of words, energy, feeling, and your intentions.

State your affirmations as if what you are putting out for has already happened or you have obtained it. Here are a few examples, but you can also make up your own. State each affirmation out loud three times with feeling.

I am happy, calm, and healthy.

I am abundant.

I am a powerful being.

I live my passion and purpose.

I am a vehicle for God to work through in assisting others.

Be creative with your affirmations. There are no limits. Repeat them every morning, even if only for two minutes, or when driving the car to work or going for a walk. Repeat each affirmation as many times as needed.

Heart and Mind Coherence Exercise

Nowadays, it is acknowledged that the heart has neurons, not just the brain. Most people work from the human mind. However, when working from the heart, you will also have access to the valuable information the brain has to offer. The heart space interfaces with the Light Body, which interfaces with the Field of Source.

While working with this in my own way, I came across Greg Braden and the HeartMath Institute. Both have done amazing, similar work by taking it to new levels in releasing trauma, among other things. I highly recommend his work and checking out the HeartMath Institute as well.

This exercise can be modified, including asking yourself questions:

1. Put your hand on your heart as a point of focus, with the intention to have a coherent relationship between your mind/brain and heart. Feel that your heart and mind are one.

2. Hold this position and breathe for at least thirty seconds (two minutes if you can manage it).

3. You might also want to send yourself love. Many think they are not worthy of love, but love for yourself first and foremost and

seeing yourself as a child of God, as well as an aspect of God, is how we start to become Creator Beings. The love frequency is a birth frequency, because all is created from love.

4. From this place, you can ask questions. If an answer is "yes," you will feel an expansion; if "no" or "not sure" compression and/or no sensation might come through. Use your intuition in terms of what feels right with the answer you receive. It could come in the form of a thought, idea, or knowingness.

This might seem simple, because it is, but doing this regular practice can transform your life and create more love for yourself and others. It will amplify the love in your life and, in effect, transform you. This has the effect of transforming and assisting others to do the same. Bring heart and mind coherence into your life.

The Buddha Smile

Close your eyes, connect within, and smile. Just be present. Do this for a minute or so. Smiling can connect you to the Divine within, shift energies, and even reset your energy. This is a very simple but effective technique.

You can even add visualizing something you did that you might not be happy about, a loved one who needs support or healing, or trauma and/or past events. Then, through thought, send love, compassion, and gratitude and be in a place of non-judgment. Release whatever it is. This is another cord-cutting type exercise.

Consider smiling as you visualize whatever you wish to manifest. You can also project and see future outcomes as if they have already happened in this way.

Heart Activation Technique

Again, imagination is creation. With this in mind breathe in and visualize Source energy coming down through the top of your head and into your heart. As you breathe out, imagine your heart space energy (the Heart Chakra) expanding and shining brightly as whatever color you intuitively feel it to be. Repeat this process until you feel you have done it enough times and shifted the energy or tapped into Source.

You could visualize the heart energy as pink, which assists with self-love, love for others, and cosmic love. Some might visualize it as green, which commonly resembles the Heart Chakra from a yogic point of view. Just use your intuition.

From this place, consider meditating on a specific decision or situation. Simply sit peacefully in heart love energy and let your answers come.

Chapter 4
GROUNDING

Connecting to the Earth can balance your energies. Perhaps you are too much in the spiritual realms or lost in your head. Connecting to the Earth can assist you with balance as you soak up positive energy from the Earth and release negative energy.

The healing benefits of grounding can help alleviate aches and pains, and heal muscles, bones, cuts, and wounds. It can also help your heart and blood, and assist with balancing them energetically to where they should be. In some cases, grounding can even help people in extreme cases, such as enable them to walk again without the need for a cane.

Grounding your energy by walking or standing barefoot on the Earth will assist with balancing your energies, bring you healing, and increase your vitality. Grounding also assists with focus and concentration, and brings about balance and good mood by resetting the mind, body, and energetic body, which reduces stress and is good for the muscles and organs. In this life, you only get one body, and taking care of it is essential to being happy, healthy, and productive.

The Earth is healing, but over the years we have become disconnected from it through concrete, the rubber on our shoes, and due to spending a lot of time indoors. Even sitting outside for five minutes in the backyard can make a difference. Connect with the Earth and be present.

Earth Grounding

Up with the sun is the way to start your day, although this can evolve on a spiritual path to where you might start to get up naturally at 2:00 to 3:30 a.m. This is something I do almost daily, and then I meditate or do yoga or other practices. I don't want to freak you out by making you think, "What, I have to get up in the early hours of the morning to be spiritual?" No, no, no! This will evolve in a way in and of itself if you choose to do so.

The sun, moon, planetary bodies, and even the star systems and where we are in the galaxy, and where our galaxy is compared to others and the other dimensions, has an influence on us. They all have their own cycles.

The sun is a giver of life in our material existence on Earth. It sustains and revitalizes us and helps plants grow. The moon also influences us because of its effects on the tides and cycles. The Earth also has a Circadian rhythm.

Getting up with the sun can be beneficial in creating routine, but discipline and determination are also needed. Waking up early can be a natural process. In a short period of time, early rising can reset the body and mind, and create a cycle of productivity. Getting outdoors even for a short amount of time is helpful, too.

Exposure to sunlight produces a serotonin boost during the day, which helps with happiness; it also produces vitamin D, which is good for your health and immune system. When the sun photons power up, the human light/energy body is greatly nourished.

Sitting or even standing outside in sunlight with your arms open as if embracing the sun, even for a minute, can help calibrate and reset your system for the rest of the day. Try doing this as the sun is rising or when it sets.

Grounding Using the Breath

Breathing can be used for grounding and for connecting to Source. There are many types of breathing exercises, including yogic Pranayama; I recommend giving all of them a go.

Prana in Sanskrit means *vital life force*, and *yama* means *control.* Many benefits can be had from breathing exercises, including raising your energy, focus, heart rate, nervous system function, and function of your digestive and immune systems. It also clears blockages in the nadis (subtle nerve channels through which prana flows).

Breathing exercises can also assist with self-realization and the attainment of psychic powers, such as Siddhis (supernatural abilities), and as a focal point for breathing in and receiving God, and breathing out and taking yourself to God. Union! Controlled breathing can lead to control of the energy distribution in your body and the cohesive relationship between the physical and energetic bodies. The love/bliss state that comes from this type of yoga assists with self-mastery as we gain control of our human body, mind, and spirit.

Self-Love

Self-love is part of the transformation and maintenance process, not just for the body, but also for the mind/body/spirit complex. Self-love is not selfish; it is not weak. It is essential for you to experience love, happiness, productivity, and the joys the world and God have to offer.

Starting each day with a little self-love can produce an energetic, clear mindset in which productivity and positivity are by-products that rub off on others, making you more effective when being of service. Loving yourself will also help you be more loving towards others. It means you will be in a better vibrational state. People and even animals will be attracted to you because of the light and the feeling of love that emanates from you. Love is a feeling, a force, an energy to be embraced. Your light will always attract love from others. When troubling situations arise, self-love will help you better handle them with a clear mind and well-rounded understanding.

Love binds us together as a human race. It connects us to others and with nature, the Earth, the universe, and God. It's our true and unbounded state. Everyone wants to be loved, happy, and healthy. This is a basic checklist for enlightenment. This is not external, but an internal state that can be found because it is always with us.

The frequency of love is a clear, powerful, sharp, high vibrating energy that is not distorted. It is productive. When you are in a love frequency, you are clear in mind, powerful, and beaming with energy. When you are not, your mind and judgment can be cloudy and distorted.

Due to the worries of the world, bills, doing this, doing that, etc, many have lost the way of self-love and care. But, in truth, if you make it a priority, your life will be a breeze, not just a thought or an action to take care of the demands placed on you. Love is our true state of being.

Science and the Mind

The science behind the mind is really not understood by today's scientists, and it's the same with energy. A balance of science and spirit is needed; they go hand-in-hand. Science helps us understand the mechanics of the mind and body. The spirit helps us understand the blueprint, the non-physical and the conscious nature and creation of our existence and reality. Together, they lead to learning more about both. Lack of understanding this has been the downfall of the human race, as in the past with Atlantis.

There have been many falls and extinctions from wars with other civilizations living here on Earth, although there are races, such as the Lemurians, Atlanteans, and others still existing in pockets *inside* the Earth, and in some cases they are also in another dimension.

The people living in Atlantis lost their way in three downfalls over several hundred thousand years. They started a war with Lemuria, created imbalance between science and spirituality, and committed despicable acts. They played "God" with genetics and eventually blew themselves up and sunk unto the ocean. Each downfall was due to an imbalance between science and spirituality.

Working together, science and spirituality help us learn about ourselves and how the world and universe work, as well as the body, mind, and spirit.

The Great Awakening

Love is the vibration that unlocks the mysteries that are not really mysteries, but they are blocked due to the lower level of consciousness that most humans are operating in when they are not in a state of love and harmony.

Love opens doors and leads to the unfolding of the knowledge within and also in the outer worlds. It's our true nature and part of our evolutionary process currently to connect with this vibration and restore balance to ourselves and the Earth. This is the time we are in now. Some call it *The Great Awakening*. Some call it *The Great Reset*. This immense change depends on what we decide to create for ourselves. Will we create a loving society that gives everyone an opportunity to live their dreams and be the best version of themselves, for themselves and the world? Or will we continue living in draconian, soul-depleting societies?

It's for us to decide. War, fighting, and arguing will not achieve peace on Earth, but through love and compassion it can be done. Love for ourselves, each other, the Earth, and God is key to the evolutionary process. Beginning each day with love for yourself and remembering this throughout the day, in time will bring about change in you and also in the world. In some cases, the effects can happen overnight.

Exercises – Tips and Tools

Basic Earth Grounding

The Earth is healing, but over the years we have become disconnected from it through concrete, the rubber on the soles of our shoes, and due to spending a lot of time indoors. Even sitting outside for five minutes in the backyard can make a difference.

There are two methods of grounding: the physical method and, let's say, the non-physical method.

With the physical method, taking off your shoes and standing or otherwise connecting to the Earth is all that's needed. You can also face the sun for added benefit.

Grounding with Hatha Yoga

The practice of yoga is usually associated with India. Designed to raise consciousness and help us reach enlightenment, there are several ways to get there. For the purposes of this book, I have mostly included hatha yoga, which is primarily yoga related to the physical body. As such, it involves physical postures called *asanas* or *poses*. In the beginning, it would be best to find a teacher in your area. Either way, with or without a teacher, start with poses for beginners and work your way up to whatever level you feel comfortable with in terms of more in-depth asanas. Taking a yoga class online, streaming online, or watching instructions on a DVD are great ways to start.

Hatha yoga has many benefits and it is popular in the Western world. It improves health and increases energy flow. It also increases personal discipline and teach us what we are capable of without overdoing it

Starting the day with even ten minutes (although I recommend twenty minutes or more, if possible) can help you start your day in a more active, yet present state with clarity and keep you in shape. It also helps digestion and your emotional state.

Try yoga in whatever way you can. It's not about going into the most far-out asanas straight away, but learning the simple poses first. Yoga can teach you what your beautiful body is capable of, along with patience and eventually self-realization. Keeping your body in shape is key to being loving and happy, so see your body as a temple and treat it with respect.

Yoga is not just about the poses, but the lifestyle and the union with your true nature, being in truth, spiritually clear, and possessing a balance of mind, body, and spirit.

The Tadasana Asana

I like to do the Tadasana yoga asana (the Mountain Pose) when grounding, but it can be done any way you choose, as long as your skin is making direct contact with the Earth. This asana is done standing straight with your arms out from your sides and your palms facing forward, big toes just touching. A little space between your heels will help with posture, balance, and the mind/body connection.

The Savasana (Corpse Pose)

This pose is similar to Tadasana, except it is done lying down with your arms at a comfortable distance from the body; thus, the name Corpse Pose. For this method of grounding, lie down on the grass or ground and simply breathe deeply and peacefully. Sitting on the ground and touching the Earth, dirt, grass, or sand can be enough.

Introduction to Breathing Exercise

This exercise is included in many meditations and yoga practices. It can bring you back to the present and it helps reduce anxiety and depression. It is a simple exercise you can do anytime, anywhere. The present moment is where all beings are magical and creative and clear.

A simple technique is to breathe in for 4 seconds, while counting 1,2,3,4. Hold for another count of 1,2,3,4, and then breathe out counting 1,2,3,4. Repeat for as long as feels comfortable. Even doing these repetitions three times can be useful.

Breath of Fire, Pranayama Exercise

This is another type of breathing exercise that can provide many benefits. It is simple, quick, and effective. It assists with oxygenating the blood, detoxifying, building, and exercising the lungs and respiratory system, and generally increases energy flow in the body.

Stop immediately if this practice makes you feel dizzy. If you have heart, blood pressure, epilepsy, strokes, or other major health issues, do not attempt this exercise.

Here are simple instructions for this exercise:

1. Sit up straight in a meditation pose.
2. Bring your chin in slightly, aligning the spine with the back of the neck.
3. Keep your eyes closed.
4. Rest your hands in a comfortable position.
5. Begin breathing in and out of your nose quickly and shallowly with an in and out rhythm, as if sniffing in and out at a comfortable pace. You might find your stomach and chest pulsating in a rhythmic manner, which serves the purpose of massaging your abdominal organs.

6. Do this for one minute or as long as you feel like it.

Healing Light Meditations

The non-physical method of grounding can be practiced with these meditations.

Connecting to Spiritual Light using a Grounding Cord

Sit in a relaxed pose with your (shoeless) feet flat on the floor and your hands in your lap, palms up. Imagine there is a cord attached to the base of your spine that goes down into the center of the Earth. This cord can be any color or thickness that feels right and it can be made of any material. Once you create your cord, it will always be available to ground you to the Earth. All you have to do is think about it. Your cord can go through solid objects, even if you are on the top floor of a tall building or flying in an airplane because it is made of energy.

Next, visualize a large ball of sparkling, golden light about a foot above your head. If another color is more appealing, use that color. Slowly and gently, bring the light down in through the top of your head. See it moving throughout your body and filling you with light: your head, throat, chest, solar plexus, and abdomen. Send it down your arms and legs, and back up to your abdomen.

Finally, send the light down through the grounding cord at the base of your spine and into the center of the Earth, taking with it any disease, illness, anxiety, anger, or other negative emotion or disturbance. This process is also called *running energy*.

Connecting to Earth Energy Using a Grounding Cord

This exercise is especially helpful when you are feeling anxious, fearful, over-stimulated, hyperactive, or just generally ungrounded.

Sit in a relaxed pose with your (shoeless) feet flat on the floor and your hands in your lap, palms up. As with the previous exercise, imagine there is a cord attached to the base of your spine that goes down into the center of the Earth.

Next, visualize a cord attached to the bottom of each foot. These cords also go down into the center of the Earth. This time, imagine there is earth energy rising up through all three cords (the one at the base of your spine and the two going into your feet).

Feel the energy enter your body and begin to rise up until it has filled you completely. This energy will feel thick and heavy, but not burdensome. After this process is complete, you might decide to move the earth energy back down through your body and out through the cord at the base of your spine, taking with it any stress or other negative influence.

Create a Protective Shield of Light

When dealing with stressful situations or troublesome people, you can protect yourself by creating an energetic shield. Simply pull your mind back a bit from the situation and visualize your body encased in a tube of white, sparkling, light. Affirm your intention that no negativity can pass through this protective shield, although you will still be able to interact with those around you. This tool can be used when you are with someone who wants to argue or who is otherwise excessively negative or annoying.

Another way to create a shield is to visualize a large sheet of white light between you and the person who is troublesome. Often this is all that is necessary to protect yourself energetically *and* help the other person calm down. After all, it can be difficult to argue with someone who just smiles at you from behind an invisible, protective shield.

Sometimes a specific chakra or part of the physical body needs protection from a person, situation, or psychic attack. In this case, you can create an energetic shield of your own design in front of your body or encircling the part of you that needs protection.

For example, imagine you are in a situation at work with a boss or co-worker and the tone of the conversation begins to make your stomach hurt. Perhaps the other person is sending anger and control energy into your third chakra. Simply create a temporary shield over your stomach to deflect the negativity. This is also useful when you are in an enclosed space such as riding in a car with a troublesome person.

Send Love to Your Heart

Place your hands in a prayer pose, palms touching in front of your heart, and focus on connecting to your heart. Bow your head and say "Namaste," which means: "The Divine within me bows to the Divine within you." In this exercise, you are bowing to yourself and the God within. This can help you get into the heart space and the Divine/God/Consciousness state. It will become second nature as a way to program your mind, body, and spirit to acknowledge and connect with the Divine.

Self-Love Exercise

Place either hand on your heart and set the intention to connect to your heart. Send love, gratitude, compassion, forgiveness, and gratitude to yourself, either through thought or by speaking out loud. Send love to your heart for every beat and whatever else comes to mind in the moment. A shift in energies can occur with this exercise that will uplift your vitality, clarify your thoughts, and elevate you spiritually.

Chapter 5
SENSING ENERGY, VIBRATION, AND SEEING THE UNSEEN

A spiritual or yogic life, if putting a label on it (actually, it's a way of being), is not just about doing asanas, meditating, wearing active-wear, and talking about love and light. These things you can do, but it doesn't make you spiritual or enlightened. Rather, the way we live is what matters.

With that said, you can do these things or not and still be following a path to Ascension if you are coming from the heart. There's a natural flow as we develop, which is key for a yogic life, enlightenment, and Ascension. Being in the flow and finding your own groove is also key.

What does the word "yoga" mean? It means union with the Source of all things – not through belief but through experiencing the Divine and your true nature.

Many yogic asanas (poses) have benefits for the energetic construct of the human vehicle, mechanics, and operating system. From the meridians to the chakras, there are literally trillions of volts running through the human body that science can measure today, but there is also the non-physical aspect.

The 8 Limbs of Yoga

The 8 Limbs of yoga are based on Patanjali's sutras. Embracing these practices and guidelines for progress on the spiritual path can assist with physical, mental, and emotional harmony, leading up to union with the Source of all things and Ascension.

1. Yamas: Self-restraints – Non-violence, truth, control of sexual urges, no stealing and no greed.

2. Niyamas: Self-observances – Contentment, self-study, austerity, purity, and devotion to Source.

3. Asanas: Physical yoga poses.

4. Pranayama: Vital energy control through breathing exercises.

5. Pratyahara: Withdrawal from the senses and disassociation from awareness of the outside environment in order to connect to the inner awareness.

6. Dharana: Concentration.

7. Dhyana: Meditation.

8. Samadhi: Union with Source.

Balancing the Chakras

Originating from the Vedas, which are ancient spiritual texts from India, the Sanskrit word *chakra* means *wheel* or *disc*. Chakras are contained within the human energy field. They are spinning energetic vortexes, portals of energetic points within and throughout the body; although at the advanced level some are outside of the body. Although some believe there are 114 chakras, we are going to focus on the basic seven. There are many books on this subject if you want to go into detail, but to work with them in a simple way is easy. By opening and activating the primary seven you can create a chain reaction unfolding the energy of all the chakras.

Over the years, people have come to me in need of assistance after seeing a practitioner or guru who worked on their chakras. Some have gone on a holiday and thought they would give energy healing a go, or they had their chakras worked on to please their partner, only to open a door they were not ready to fathom or deal with due to their position in the evolutionary process.

All the chakras, for the most part, should not be unlocked without doing the inner work, as this can be very unproductive for some. They can lose structure in daily life and have confusing experiences as a result of tapping into the multidimensional aspect of existence without grounding.

Coming to me for help in this type of situation has happened on the odd occasion, and rebalancing of the chakras has been necessary, but not to shut them down. Through feeling, sensation, and over years of training, practices, and following my intuition and guidance from different Masters on and off-world, I have come to be able to help people find balance within both their physical body and the mental, emotional, astral/energetic aspects of the Light Body and blueprint construct of human existence, including the Tree of Life and Merkabah construct.

Balance is needed in all things! You see, the physical body and the non-physical aspect run at optimal efficiency in a cohesive manner when they are in balance. At times, we go through a growth period and we evolve, build up, and advance, but along the way balance in the evolutionary process is key.

An analogy I like use is to tune the chakras like an instrument. Balancing them is part of self-mastery, as well as self-inquiry with regard to your emotions and feelings and doing the mirror and shadow work. Mental health and physical health are connected and affect one another. Sometimes, where we think our problems lie can actually be a manifestation from many different points in the physical and non-physical bodies and/or negative influences or entities.

Instead of "Be careful what you wish for" ask yourself, "Am I ready for what I wish for?" Discipline and dissolving the ego need to be addressed on the spiritual path, as well.

Becoming Buddha

So often, people think they can train with a teacher, guru, or Master and become a Master themselves overnight. The Master is already within. You are a Master, but reconnecting with the true nature of self and the work that comes with it is a journey in and of itself that cannot be fast-tracked.

Any teacher is first and foremost a student; all are in a state of learning. Even when we are enlightened, learning about our own inner mechanics and the working of the inner and outer worlds is necessary. Service to others also comes into play in a way that is deeper than before through means tailored by our experience and knowledge. In this way, we learn from each other.

No one is above or below you. We are each a drop in the ocean of consciousness and all knowledge of the ocean is within each drop. We are one in the body of God but we experience that oneness from different aspects and points of awareness, which is why the illusion of separateness sometimes seems so real. It's all about learning and gleaning knowledge for the overall collective.

Happiness, health, and just being a good person are the basics of living a spiritual life. So often we take something easy and simplistic and make it complicated. Simple can still be useful and effective.

Some travel the world going to ashrams and spiritual retreats, and from guru to guru, only to find in the end that everything they needed was within them all along. Believe me, these places are great to experience, but sometimes we are not at a stage to understand what's within us, which is why some go from place to place seeking spiritual enlightenment outside of themselves. Nevertheless, traveling for spiritual experience is part of the journey because we are accumulating knowledge that will eventually unlock the knowledge already within us. It's still a worthwhile process.

Here's a little story from Mullah Nasrudin of India. Parables such as this are a fun way to illustrate spiritual concepts such as the need to look within.

> Once there was a musk deer who noticed a heavenly, delicious scent in the air.

Intoxicated, she set out to the find the source of the divine aroma. She searched everywhere, but it eluded her. She searched every forest and field and town, but she couldn't find the source of the scent. She just *knew* she would not be happy until she found it.

Then one day she fell exhausted onto the forest floor, and as she fell one of her own horns pierced her own belly.

Suddenly, the air was flooded with the divine heavenly scent. After a lifetime of searching, she realized the scent was coming from inside of her the whole time.

Meeting gurus and Masters, and visiting spiritual places can be great for learning and meeting like-minded others, as well as learning tips and tools. And yes, some have the effect of activating us. Initiations can take place and assist in our evolutionary process. Masters can activate and download knowledge and teachings, and so can ancient places, power spots, and ethereal and crystal libraries located all over the world.

Many of these unseen, inter-dimensional libraries of knowledge and intelligences intersect with sacred places on Earth. They draw us to them, not knowing why we must go there or meet a certain person – only for it to actually make sense after the fact when connecting the dots.

There is much happening on the astral planes, but you will eventually understand that even in the darkness, the light you are looking for has been within you all along. My purpose is to help you know the light is within, as well as assist with some tools and food for thought to help you find, unlock, and reconnect with what's within you waiting to be revealed. My purpose is to help empower you as you walk the path and find your own "book of the soul," written by and contained within your Higher Self. We all have our own "book," and it must be (and is) different from that of others. We are Creator Beings inside the Master Creator that is experiencing itself.

Unlocking the chakras, opening the Third Eye, following your intuition, and doing it all in a joyful state is the path, but self-inquiry comes into play first. Whether your troubles have been caused by trauma, wrong conclusions, or poor judgment, it is never too late to release the past and find forgiveness. Take control of your path and create the reality you desire.

Don't be surprised if teachers, Masters and/or otherworldly Beings present themselves to you during this awakening process. Some of you might feel you need help from a counselor, a psychologist, or a spiritual teacher. It is important that you do not feel alone when your mind and world are shaken by an awakening experience. This can change everything, and we all need help sometimes.

When you do get help, and most of all help yourself, you will be in awe of what you are capable of and the inner mechanics of the journey. Embrace it and understand that you and your experiences are aspects of The Creator. It's just a matter of time until you reconnect with the Master within and remember the mechanics of the outer and inner worlds. Understanding the mechanics of your body, mind, and energetic blueprint is the way to go.

The point is that all of us are at different stages and have different levels and ways of understanding our reality, whether in a complex way – or not. This is what you have to work with. There is no right or wrong, or better or worst way; it is what it is.

Basic methods are effective, which if understood can lead to what at the earlier stages might have seemed like complex practices, understanding, and knowledge. Understanding prana/chi to start with is a great introductory and effective way of mastering your experience. Recognize and feel it within yourself and then work with your own energies.

Even changing your mood and acknowledging how you feel can change the energetic body and give you a reference point from where you were to where you are now, and also to where you can go. As below, so above, and vice versa. Creators we are. As you work with your energies of both a physical and non-physical nature, much can be unlocked. Not just knowledge, being of service, love, joy, abilities, balance, physical and mental health, and happiness, but at some point the multidimensional mind starts to kick in and blend with your perception of this physical world.

For example, you might see flashes of light, which could be higher dimensional Beings such as Angels, enlightened extraterrestrials, orbs, portals, and the like. You might encounter Shadow Beings, misty and smoky manifestations, apparitions, fairies, elementals, Bigfoot, or even another aspect of yourself. It's game on, up to and including physical manifestations and visions.

Many people do not have knowledge or experience in these matters, nor is it talked about in terms of educating people in spiritual communities. In most spiritual settings, when a teacher is asked by a student about an experience they had with a UFO, ET, Shadow Being, or Light Being, etc., the teacher is likely to say something like, "We don't talk about that." Spiritual teachers can be prone to doing this because they know all answers lie within, but also because their teacher and the teacher's teacher and so on, were always told either to say, "We don't talk about that," or "It's a distraction from going within."

Many teachers from around the world have confided in me privately and shared their experience. They ask questions because they are trying to understand what they experienced. If their knowledge is limited as to the nature of multidimensional mind and communication, they will not understand that the more you evolve, the more the intelligences comprising the greater family of man start to interact with you, of both a positive and negative nature, depending on perception. A lot of the time they are old friends from other existences and/or the person is becoming psychic or always has been, but the teacher is telling them not to acknowledge their own experience. In some cases, the teacher might not even recognize that the student is naturally gifted as a seer, a person who is capable of seeing beyond what most can perceive in the physical dimension. The student might not even know it themselves.

This is not to have a dig at anyone, but to educate you about what I have learned, which is that many people do not understand their experiences. They are looking for answers, which is a natural process, and progression. A Master Being can interact with you as a guide and assist in your evolutionary process and understanding of multidimensional realities and teachings.

Years ago, I wanted to bring the UFO, paranormal, science, health, and spiritual communities together, and over the years I have seen them merge more and more. Truly, everything is connected. Yes, all answers are within, but if you lack understanding and education or if you are fixated on a specific position, your answer might be blocked. Otherworldly Beings are not to be looked up to; humans must see themselves as equals. As we evolve collectively and individually, we need to understand that when we are communicating with guides, ETs, etc., they are only middlemen. Like a family or friend, you take their advice or you don't. A real friend will accept you. An enemy will guilt trip you. The information or experience of a trickster will make no sense.

It comes back to the fruit of the information. To be enlightened is to be in possession of all the knowledge you can be at your stage of evolution. This is why I am sharing this. If any practices or ways of learning have already been discovered and they are considered the *only* way, there would be no need for this book or any books or spiritual teachers, practices, and techniques, because everything would already be known.

The way in which the human body responds to thoughts and feelings has been forgotten, too. Over time, I started to acknowledge this more and more, not just multidimensionally in terms of contact and communication, but to the point of checking in with my own body, the organs and the cells of my body. It's a simple check-up using intuition.

This also led to working with the Light Body and shielding myself from other influences. At the very basic level, I recognized and learned to feel safe with my abilities as an empath. Personally, I believe most, if not all, people have the traits and ability to be empathetic, and this is amplified as you evolve on the spiritual path.

Basically, given that all is connected, everything has a cause and effect, and everything and everyone is at its/their own stage in evolution. This needs to be respected. It needs to be taken seriously, not in an obsessive or unproductive manner, but in a loving and accepting matter, and by being objective and productive when possible.

In the end, all will be revealed to the student when the student is ready. Likewise, the teacher appears when the student is ready to unlock his or her inner knowingness.

The Energy Bodies

As discussed throughout this book, we are more than just the physical body, and as we progress on the path of Ascension, we come to understand each of the energy bodies in succession. This brief but useful description of the aspects of what and who we are is slightly different from what is commonly known and accepted, because I collaborated with James Gilliland on this from the point of view of our own experience and guidance.

> Physical Body – The *Temple of Consciousness* necessary to experience Earth reality.
>
> Mental Body – Thoughts, memory, and information.
>
> Emotional Body – Feeling and emotions.
>
> Astral Body – Energetic body.
>
> Etheric Body – Light Body.
>
> Spiritual Body – Wave function body.
>
> I AM Body – Higher Self, the Cell of Source we all are.
>
> Cosmic Body – In harmony with Source/God/Creator.

Self Mastery – The Path to Ascension

Exercises – Tips and Tools

Sensing Energy

We feel energy coming towards us from outside of us all the time, but it often goes unnoticed. When you get goose bumps, your hair stands on end, or you feel temperature changes, vibrations, or a tingling sensation, it could mean there is another intelligence in your presence. This might be a Spirit Guide, a saint, sage, Master, ET, Angel, or even Yeshua or Buddha. It could be Source or your own spiritual energy being activated or upgraded, or you are receiving a download of multidimensional information. You might even be sensing the vibration of the reality these other Beings are currently experiencing. Try this exercise to help you get acquainted with energy and the sensation of it coming into you:

Rub your hands together back and forth very quickly for fifteen seconds. Then hold your hands about half a foot from each other in front of you.

The rubbing creates heat from friction and a sensation, but then there is a vibration that momentarily allows you to feel the energy. This is a very easy technique that yogis and Masters use sometimes to build up energy, as well as create a focal point for directing energy.

The more you play with this technique, the more you will notice energetic changes naturally when they happen and/or when you are in the presence of an unseen intelligence, when doing healing, or when you are in an area with different energy. Sometimes, this is felt from your feet to half-way up your shins and sometimes to higher parts of the body, or even your whole body when you are in a vortex, portal, or high energy location.

Vipassana Meditation / Sensing Vibrations

Vipassana meditation was first taught by Buddha. This practice teaches us to see reality as it really is: a way of self-observation and self-transformation. Vipassana explores the interconnectedness between the mind and body using discipline and paying attention to physical sensations.

To do Vipassana meditation, simply follow your breath. Observe with detachment the air flowing in and out of your nose. This is often done in a retreat setting for ten or more hours a day over three or ten days.

After a while, you will notice a vibration under your nose above your top lip (this is always going on). Once you notice this sensation, begin to focus your awareness on a certain part of your body. Soon you will become aware that this part is vibrating, too. Then, as you begin to work your way from your legs to the top of your body, you will notice that whatever part of your body you are focusing on is vibrating. The vibrating is constant. After a few days in silence, focusing on your breath and the vibration in your body, you will start to go beyond the five-sense reality.

Vibrating in this three-dimensional reality, you can play with rising and lowering it, which can allow you to experience other realms and what usually goes unseen. This aspect isn't necessarily taught in Vipassana Meditation and it should be undertaken with guidance from a reliable teacher in a retreat setting.

Learning about Auras

Auras are produced by the light emanating from within the bodies of all living creatures, including the plant and animal kingdoms. Everyone has the innate ability to see them. Sometimes, we see auras in our Mind's Eye, our inner vision, in which case our eyes are not necessarily open.

For some, the specific color of the aura correlates to the person's emotions and the energetic state of the person being seen. The aura sometimes shows blockages, although I suggest going by intuition as to what you sense when tuning into your aura or the aura of someone else.

It all depends on the person, but to physically see an aura is very simple. This ability can be enhanced over time if practiced on a regular basis.

Exercise One

Select a plain background like a wall or a table that is painted one color.

Spread your fingers apart and put your hand in front of you, with your hand a few inches away from the surface of the wall or table.

Gaze lightly at one of your fingers for about twenty seconds. Without changing your focus, you will notice what appears to be like a heat wave coming off a road on a hot day slightly around your finger. Now shift your focus to looking directly at it. This is your own aura.

For some, an aura will fade quickly, but the more you do this exercise, the longer you will be able to see it. Over time, try looking at another finger and go from finger to finger, and you will see it more. After learning this technique, you can start to see the aura energy around objects and other people.

It can intensify and color can come with it as you start to see the energy of the aura. You can play with this technique even when you are in bed with your feet in front of you turned upward or sticking out from under the sheets.

Exercise Two

Ask someone to sit on a chair or stand in front of a blank wall facing you. Then sit or stand about 3 to 5 feet away from the person at eye level. Gaze at the middle of the person's forehead. Sometimes dull lighting in your peripheral vision can enhance this experience.

After some time, you might start to notice a slight halo around the person's head and shoulders. This can intensify with practice.

When you are in the presence of someone who is evolved spiritually, you might see the person's aura without trying to.

This happens to me when I am in the presence of some humans and off-world intelligences. The experience has intensified over the years, especially from doing exercises and practices to sharpen these types of natural abilities.

Exercise Three

Another way to become sensitive to the human aura is to start by placing your hands about twelve inches from another person's head. Move your hands slowly towards the body until you feel a change in the energy emanating from the person. Next, move your hands down the sides and front of the body, and back (if the person is standing). Look for any changes in the shape or feel of the aura. If you are able to visualize using your second sight, watch for changes in color. This exercise can be refined to focus on any of the primary chakras in the body.

The Seven Primary Chakras

ROOT CHAKRA – Muladhara. Color red and located at the base of the spine. Assists with feeling secure, grounding, and stability.

SACRAL CHAKRA – Swadhisthana. Color orange and located at the lower abdomen. Assists with well-being, emotions, abundance.

SOLAR PLEXUS CHAKRA – Manipur. Color yellow and located at the upper abdomen. Assists with self-worth, confidence, esteem, and power.

HEART CHAKRA – Anahata. Color green and located in the middle of the chest. Assists with love, compassion, joy, and inner peace.

THROAT CHAKRA – Vishuddha. Color blue and located at the throat area. Assists with communication, expression, creativity, truth, and inspiration.

THIRD EYE CHAKRA – Ajna. Color indigo located in the middle of the head just above the eyes. Assists with wisdom, intuition, imagination, and visions.

CROWN CHAKRA – Sahasrara. Color violet located at the top of the crown of the head. Assists with Connection to Source, the Divine, knowledge, and consciousness.

Exploring the Chakras

As you review the list of chakras and tune into your intuition, you will understand which chakras you need to focus on first. Alternatively, start at the root chakra and work your way up.

Exercise One: Exploring the Chakras with Another Person

Hold your hands over each chakra area for a few minutes, first in front of the body, then behind (if the person is standing). Look for different energy sensations and colors, especially dark colors. Pay attention to where you can feel energy leaving your hands or projecting from the person. Notice any areas where there is no sensation, which indicate stagnation and/or illness.

With practice, this exercise can lead you to an understanding of what parts of another person's body need loving attention.

Exercise Two: Exploring Your Own Chakras

Lie down and get comfortable. Then set the intention to tune into and calibrate your chakras. From this point, visualize each chakra using your intuition and inner vision to make it brighter or duller in color, and/or expand its size or shrink it. It's very important not to open them all or shut them down, but to proceed with feeling when doing this as to how bright and big each chakra should be. When you are done with one, shift your attention to the next one. At the end, remain lying down and relax until you feel like getting up.

Self Mastery – The Path to Ascension

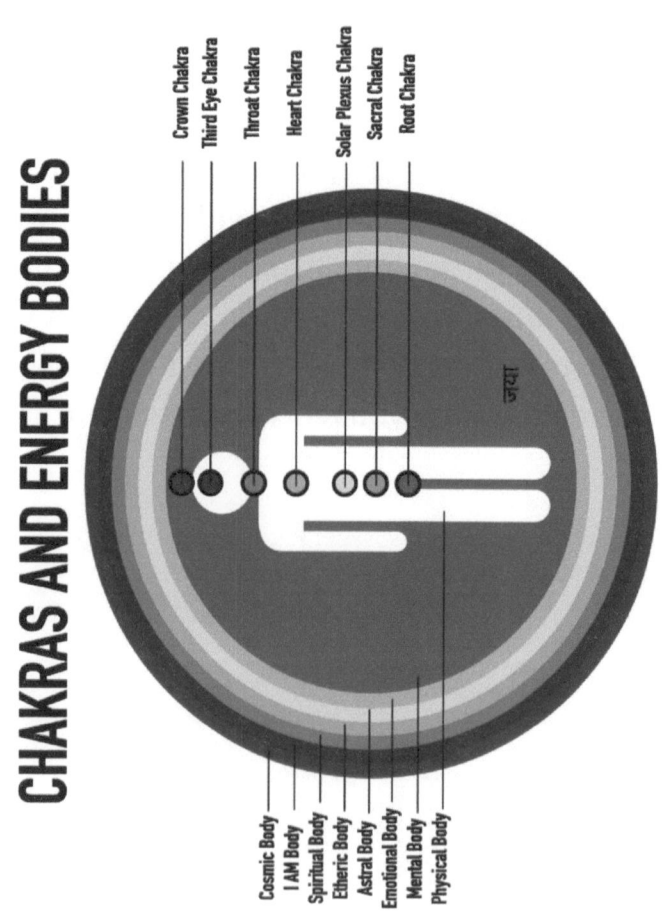

Healing and Releasing Blocks in the Chakras

These techniques use scanning with your hands and following your intuition.

Exercise One: Scanning

Bring your hands together as if holding a ball of energy and focus on activating Source energy. Through intuition, use whichever hand you feel inclined towards. Those of you who are sensitive will feel a tingling or other sensation and/or heat in your hands.

Now, scan your body, or someone else's body if you have permission or have been asked to assist with healing. Start about an inch above the body and scan until you feel a dull spot. This could be blocked energy that is not flowing properly.

Leave your hand in the dull area and ask Source energy to flow into that area until you feel the dull energy recede and the energy intensify back to a brighter, more normal level.

Another thing you can do is put your hand over the root chakra and work your way up. Set the intention for Source energy to assist each chakra in being where it needs to be energetically. By playing with this, you will recognize the sensations that feel right. You (or the person you're scanning) should end up feeling a comfortable tingling heat in the area of the body that corresponds to each chakra.

Exercise Two: Gaining Sensitivity

In order to become sensitive to the human chakras, start by placing your hands about twelve inches from another person's head. Move your hands in slowly towards the body until you can feel a change in the energy emanating from the person. Next, move your hands down the sides and front of the body (and back if the person is standing). Look for any changes in the shape or feel of the chakras. If you can visualize using your second sight, watch for changes in color. This exercise can be refined to focus on any of the main chakras in the body.

Hold your hands over each chakra area for a few minutes – first in front of the body and then behind (if the person is standing). Look for different energy sensations and colors, especially dark colors. Pay attention to where you feel energy leaving your hands and also projecting towards you from the person. Also notice areas where there is no sensation, which indicates stagnation and/or illness. With practice, this exercise can lead you to an understanding of what parts of another person's body need loving attention. Learning to heal energetically is like playing a musical instrument; the more you practice the more you *can* do it.

Seeing the Unseen Lamp Exercise

This somewhat advanced exercise is fun for those who are open to seeing otherworldly intelligences and Beings.

Sit in your lounge-room with a salt lamp or electric lamp to the side. It should be bright enough to see the whole room. First, do a Clearing to set your intention to connect with a Spirit Guide, ET, Master, or whatever is in alignment with you and needs to (or would like to) come through and make contact with you. Take care and be specific as to what or who you ask to make contact with.

Relax and don't try to control this exercise. As you continue to hold your intention, start talking like you are having a conversation with someone who is physically present. Keep it fun and try to forget

Self Mastery – The Path to Ascension

about what you are doing, while still holding your intention.

You might notice misty, smoky forms or flashes of light that blink in and out. As an example of how quickly this can happen, let's say there are thirty frames a second like there are with some videos. For example, a Being might blink in for three frames out of the thirty very quickly because they are doing their best to lower their higher frequency to ours.

Having someone with you is a way of confirmation if both of you see the same thing. Most likely one of you will say, "Did you see that?" as events take place. If others see the same thing, no one can say it's a trick of the imagination.

Make sure the blinds are closed to discount car lights and reflections, and do a Clearing before proceeding. I came up with this technique because it happens at my house when I'm alone, and it also happens when other people are with me and they see the same thing. It is easier at night, but it can happen at any time.

For more information on making contact such as this, I recommend using the "Connect to your Spirit and ET Guides" technique in the book I wrote with the same name. This book also contains a useful meditation technique that can help you learn to interface with other intelligences and Beings.

As always, if you are open to taking things to this level do a Clearing first. This exercise is best done with respect for the Beings you are hoping to contact.

Seeing the Unseen Staring Technique

Go outside with a friend and sit on separate chairs, both facing the same direction.

Look at a tree, bush, building or other solid, unmoving object at least 10 to 15 feet away and do a Clearing.

Stare at the object with an unfocused gaze for five minutes while you set your intention to connect with a Spirit Guide, ET, Master, or otherworldly Being who is in alignment with you and needs to (and would like to) come through. Don't try to control your experience; just keep it fun. Again, you might see a flash of light, an orb, smoky misty forms, or an apparition manifest.

I once did this with a friend who was a very skeptical scientist. For a moment, a smoky form appeared in front of us and materialized into an aboriginal with white circles and wavy lines painted on his chest area. When I described the form to the scientist, the scientist nearly fell off his chair. He had seen the same form with the same paint and clothing. This is best done respectfully and not abused. Always be sure to do a Clearing before attempting this exercise, and afterwards if necessary.

Chapter 6
MANIFESTING

We are Creator Beings and, as such, we create our experience here in the physical dimension. The art and practice of manifesting involves co-creating with the universe, Source, and your Higher Self in order to turn your dreams and goals into reality. So, what do you want to create?

How do you measure success? I have met many people with lots of money, nice cars, big houses, a loving partner, kids, and a holiday house. They are living the dream, but even in blessed situations they are unhappy. They don't realize they have created an unfulfilling life. The answers are staring them in the face, even though the key to unlocking the door to find answers is right inside all of us. Through passion you find purpose and with this comes abundance, including abundance beyond financial. It also has the by-product of being of service to others. It's so simple.

All who become successful have failed many times before, and their failure has been the path that led them to success. It's like a road up a mountain.

Don't let fear of the unknown and your need for security hold you back from going to the top. Embrace spiritual discipline and proceed with determination. Train your mind to focus on positive intentions, because whatever you focus on will be made manifest in your life. What you believe and focus on will be drawn to you. So take care to be mindful of your thoughts and stop yourself if your thoughts are negative, especially if they are self-critical.

You see, there are many paths up a mountain. Some paths are easier than others and there are ups and downs on all paths as you ascend or descend. Depending on the terrain, your life experience and mindset can determine how your journey will unfold in terms of development, speediness, and energy. It isn't about doing it overnight, but doing it right, which can be easily achieved by following your heart. You can cheat others and think you got away with it, but you cannot cheat yourself or God and have riches given to you on a silver platter.

How each individual feels and takes in the view at the peak will be different. We each have our own perspective while we are experiencing Earth reality. Each person's journey is unique, and the journey assists with shaping and molding their identity and the assistance they can give to humanity, the Earth, and the universe as a whole. This is part of why we leave Source to experience God from within.

Be concise in your intentions about what you want to manifest. If your intention is strong and focused, and the reason behind your intention is positive, it is likely you will achieve your goal. Let go of any limiting beliefs and decide to be happy. Believe in yourself. You can either walk this journey in a blissful state or with a bitter taste in your mouth.

Take a course, learn something new, and take chances. Follow your heart, and if you don't know why you are doing something, know that whatever you are doing it's okay as long as it doesn't harm another living being.

Everything has a cause and effect, and your actions will be your legacy, your energetic imprint on the universe. Your deeds in the blueprint of the universe are never forgotten. Your thoughts and actions will never go unnoticed.

There will come a time when you must take the next step with faith, so make positive choices that create big change. Manifest your dreams today, in ten years, or eventually when the time is right. There is a chance in every moment to be the change you want to see in the world. Just have faith; trust in God and the process. Doing what you are passionate about is key. Your positive attitude and living a life of service will also assist the collective.

Everyone has something unique they can contribute to the world. We can teach each other and be of service, and when you walk down that path with positive intentions it can be so exciting.

The point is what do you want to do? What do you want to manifest for yourself, your family, and the world? Do what you love; therein lies the answer. Through love and positive intentions, you can set yourself firmly on the path to spiritual evolution, illumination, and eventual Ascension.

Exercises – Tips and Tools

Make a Vision Board

Creating your own vision board is a great way to help manifest what you want to change or bring into your life. Starting with a thought as a focal point, your vision board can assist with fast-tracking your desire for change into physical existence. It's a visual reminder of what you want to manifest.

Take a magazine or other printed material and cut out images you feel attracted to. This might be your dream home, images of places you would like to visit, smiling faces, or an image of yourself happy. You could use a photo of someone you love to bring in loving energy. Now glue or tape the images you've chosen to a large piece of cardboard or paper.

When you are finished, tack your vision board to a wall next to your bed so it's the first thing you see in the morning, or somewhere else where you will see it on a regular basis.

When waking up each morning and before going to bed, meditate on it and visualize all of your manifestations happening in the present moment. You will be amazed as you start ticking off everything on the vision board as it becomes your reality.

Affirmations

As I've written in previous chapters, setting your intentions using affirmations can be done during meditation. First thing in the morning is best. You can also write down your goals or speak them out loud. Express your intentions and affirmations as if what you want to manifest already exists. For example: "I have love and receive it." And+ "I have a job with supportive co-workers."

Visualizing and Feeling

These practices can assist you with the manifestation process. They will help you develop your Mind's Eye abilities (your inner vision, or clairvoyance) and get your creative flow going.

Many say they can't visualize. Well, let's see. For a moment, imagine that your car or a piece of clothing is a different color. It's as simple as that.

Another way you can strengthen your ability is to feel it as you try to visualize something. Focus on the emotional feeling that comes with what you want to manifest in the present moment.

Now take thirty seconds and focus on one specific goal you would like to achieve. Feel it and see it in the now. Do this once a day with regard to a specific goal and you might be surprised with the results.

Imagine, Ground, and Manifest

With this process, visualize, feel and/or use your imagination to focus on one thing you want to manifest. This exercise should be done while standing barefoot on the ground.

Imagine using the Earth as a giant crystal to assist with your manifesting process in the physical world. Direct your intention, towards feeling and seeing that which you are putting out for in the now. This you are doing from the light blueprint. This "blueprint" is the place from which consciousness creates the physical world and everything we experience. As above, so below.

Even spending one minute a day on this exercise can produce great results.

Short- and Long-Term Goals

Sit down with a pencil and paper, or a notepad on your computer, phone, or other device.

Put your hand on your heart and call upon your Higher Self and Source. Ask to be shown whatever is for your highest good. What would you like to experience, achieve, and/or manifest with passion and purpose in the short-term, which means the next few months to a year. Write down what comes to mind.

Next, do the same for the long-term, the next 5 to 10 years. As you are writing, you are putting energy into your manifesting process and creating your vision. There is no limit. The only person who can limit you is yourself.

I recommend coming back to this exercise on a regular basis and being open to making changes in your intentions. We all go through developments and upgrades in our cycles and soul evolution, so don't be surprised if you take out and add things on a regular basis.

Surrender to Source

Following on from the above exercises, I recommend making a copy of your written goals and keeping it on your computer, or keep two written copies. Revise your goals every three months or whenever it feels right.

I also recommend burning one of the copies and letting the ashes dissolve into the ether as a way to give it to Source. Surrender and allow Source to meet you halfway. You could also put the ashes into a flowing stream.

You might choose to do this on dates that are significant to you, such as the 8/8 Lion's Gate, or on 10/10 or 11/11. Just follow your intuition. This can also be done during a full moon or on an equinox or solstice if you are so inclined. Energy flows where attention goes.

Chapter 7
THE ZONE

If you engage in physical activity such as running, swimming, or even dancing, you know the peaceful place you can reach. It's a state of mind in which you are at peace, no worries, just the rhythm of movement and physical activity. Hobbies, such as sewing, cooking, reading, and listening to music can also produce the same relaxed feeling. It's a state of daydreaming, like when you are in school looking out the window or when driving a car and time flies by. This state of being can put you into a higher state of consciousness in which great spiritual growth can be experienced. I call it *The Zone*.

The most sophisticated device in the material world you are using right now is the human body. Much is still unknown about the body, but yogis, lamas, and spiritual Masters provide examples of how truly amazing humans are and what God has created, as well as what we are capable of, not just in the material world but multidimensionally.

Navigated by your consciousness you have access to the many mansions, which allows you to experience your innate capabilities and nature beyond what can be perceived in the visible light spectrum. The word *mansion* here refers to the Biblical quote, "In my father's house there are many mansions…." John 14:2. In the context discussed in this book, "mansion" could be taken to mean the levels of multidimensional reality.

From levitation to being able to materialize objects through creative thought and being able to teleport, bi-locate, and manipulate matter, connecting to the Master within is the key to opening and unlocking your true abilities.

Get in the Zone with Physical Exercise

Through exercises and other practices, these abilities and more can become second nature. All is connected, and unfolding your true nature starts with intention. Nothing external can help you unlock your unbounded abilities and nature, although a knowledgeable teacher can help with tips and tools.

As a child, the start of this for me was going to a Karate Dojo. For years my father was teaching a style of karate known as *Gōjū-ryū* an average of three days a week. This style comes from Okinawa, Japan. Both my mom and dad are fit and disciplined, and we are lucky these traits rubbed off on my brother and me.

I practiced karate on and off throughout the first twenty years of my life, although not on a regular basis. Since then for nearly twenty years, three days a week I have practiced five Katas, solo karate moves, steps, and different types of strikes, stances, and blocks. Karate continues to assist me with coordination, discipline, breathing, and strength.

Spiritual Practice While Blindfolded

In my younger days doing karate, sometimes I would put on a blindfold and find another student as an exercise, and other times practice moves. Wearing a blindfold as a form of practice can sharpen the senses. I did this quite a bit as a child, although more so at home than in the Dojo. Now I continue to meditate and do other practices while blindfolded. This is not done for show, but something I naturally carried through the years because I believe being blindfolded assists with unlocking, enhancing, and developing sensory perception beyond the five-sense reality. It also enhances intuition, balance, feeling, and telepathic abilities.

Get in the Zone with Swimming

Swimming as a child and going to the pool with my father has helped me greatly. Some say swimming laps is the best form of exercise because the whole body gets a workout. I even won a medal or two as a kid, but it wasn't that I really wanted to be competitive; I just enjoyed it. Even on days when I didn't feel like swimming laps, I would just jump in and have fun splashing around. Swimming is so grounding and good for the body and spirit.

Swimming also helps with knee and joint problems, breathing issues, and cardio stamina. Swimming can also assist with cleansing the physical and non-physical bodies if done in a natural creek, river, or ocean. If you do not have access to flowing, natural water, an Epsom salt bath is the next best thing.

On the Subject of Discipline

The discipline I learned during my education and upbringing has helped shape the practice schedule I follow today. Exercise and spiritual practice are keys on the self-mastery path and I am blessed to have always had some structure in this way. What I am trying to relay here is do whatever exercise or practice is exciting and fun, but not if it feels like a chore. No matter what physical limitations you might have, you can start slow and easy and build up your strength. Over time, consistent practice will make your chosen practices second nature, strengthen your reactions and reflexes, and sharpen your mind, inner strength, and health. Repetition easily puts a person in The Zone, a place out of mind and worry.

Some yoga masters only practice and refine one asana for a couple of hours a day, although they are highly trained in most if not all areas in their style. This type of determination and discipline results in perfection and health in body and mind.

Find Your Own Way

The smell of a flower, the touch of another, the joy of love, the fresh air of nature, the rain and sun on your skin, the breeze on your face – these experiences make it easy to find The Zone within yourself. We live in an amazing reality, and fine-tuning our senses through exercise and experiencing the mind, body, and spirit connection helps with longevity and keeps us moving through the world with optimal efficiency.

Even walking or going for a hike in nature is good for the soul. For many, insights, guidance, and even communication in a higher state of consciousness can come through when we are in The Zone. We need only reach for and acknowledge it.

Some people think they can't meditate, which is also key, but swimming laps can be the equivalent. Even walking or doing crossword puzzles can be meditation for some people. When you are in The Zone, you can connect to higher intelligences because your mind, body, and spirit are in cohesive relationship.

Daydreaming is another way of experiencing The Zone. We have all done it, especially as children. In The Zone, downloads of spiritual information, answers, insight, concepts, epiphanies, a knowingness, and blueprints about the nature of the universe can come through. This experience is beyond conversation and linear mind. Anyone can experience it, but if they are trapped in a material world or not open or educated on this type of experience, they might pass it off as mere fantasy.

Thoughts create reality and imagination is also creation. In some cases, scientists and inventors are experiencing revelations, solving problems, and creating from this space. In The Zone and while daydreaming, and even in the dream time, we go multidimensional and receive insight and communication. My point is, finding your zone and what gets you into the stillness of it is key. The state of no mind is being within God's mind.

Find your own way to enter The Zone. From this state of being, the higher mind will unfold and reveal your true nature, which is beyond the physical. It can be experienced momentarily, but with the discipline of finding your Zone, over time you will be able to tap into it at any time. All of your answers and knowledge can be found in the Zone.

Spending time in The Zone is about your relationship with yourself, which also means your relationship with God and with others. If your relationships are right within and with God, the rest will be right, too.

As we travel the path to Ascension, the answers come and the unseen reveals itself in all its brilliance.

Self Mastery – The Path to Ascension

Exercises – Tips and Tools

Spend Time in Nature

One way you can experience a glimpse of multidimensional mind is to get out into nature. It's amazing what can happen in nature at the most subtle and noticeable levels.

Being out in nature is grounding. The fresh air, the wildlife, and the beauty are uplifting. It can reset you emotionally and energetically. Also, it assists with connecting to Source and your Higher Self to receive answers and insight. Let me give you an example.

Let's say you wake up in the morning and you are working on a project, but by midday you have gotten nowhere with it and you need a break. So, you decide to go for a half an hour walk. Fifteen minutes into the walk, you are in The Zone, that state of mind in which all is forgotten and the mind chatter stops. Answers and revelations to fix or solve the issues you were dealing with earlier come flowing into your consciousness, at which point you rush on home and do whatever you were trying to do in a heartbeat. And then it's done!

The place of no mind is God's Mind and it's incredibly vast.

Now where does the information come from? It could be God/Source, the Higher Self, Spirit Guides, a Master, an Angel, another aspect of self that's fractal from the godhead aspect, an ET, Bigfoot, or even a Fairy Being.

The point is you had an intention for a long time and then you let go and got out of your own way. As your mind goes into The Zone and your mind chatter dissolves, ideas, epiphanies, knowingness, and imagination will come to you as you connect to the field. It's like doing psychokinesis and you are able to move objects with your mind. But that's a subject for another time.

Always do what works for you, but just being in nature and in some cases doing an activity in a natural setting can help you connect to your true unbounded state.

Yoga

As previously discussed, yoga can be an enjoyable, challenging, rewarding, and uplifting spiritual practice. But it's not just about doing hatha yoga postures. Rather, it's a discipline, a way of life, a way to improve fitness. Yoga assists with the maintenance of the body, uplifting and balancing out your energies, sculpting the body, as well as balancing out and connecting the mind, physical body, and energetic body.

It's amazing how breathing through the postures, feeling the energy, the openings and closing of areas in the body, and learning what the body is capable of can stretch your limits. The push to endure and go beyond what you *believe* to be your limitations can connect you to higher consciousness. It can also open blockages and kinks in your energetic flow and wiring, bringing you into an amazing state of mind, body, and spirit connection. However, if you are not motivated to do this or any of the exercises in this book, don't force it. Just try giving it a go and be open.

You see, it's not just the postures, the breathing, or the mindset, but the mind expansion experience that comes with it. Yoga is a way of life, but don't stay in the box of the commercial aspect of it. Expand your practice and allow yourself to be led to other worlds and other realms. Yoga is a vast subject and collection of practices beyond what is known within the commercial aspect.

Qigong

The precursor to Tai Chi, Qigong is an ancient Chinese practice that brings flow, energy, grounding, clarity, and a mind-opening experience. It's like yoga, but in its own way.

The Dantians are energy points (or centers) in the energy body; they are divided into upper, lower, and middle. They are different from the chakras in that they are another level of the energetic vortexes within the Light Body overlapping the physical body. Qigong has many practical exercises and I highly recommend it. It can be as complicated or enjoyable as you want, but doing a few classes or even following an online video can be enjoyable and educational, and lead to a spiritual experience.

Just like yoga, meditation, and many other spiritual practices, before beginning, gauge the energy in your body and how you feel, and then again afterwards. You might be surprised by the difference.

What I am saying here is you don't *have* to do yoga, karate, or any other practice. None of this is mandatory for self-growth. Yes, I do, but I want you to find what works for you. Whether you do several different practices or one, just do something and enjoy it.

The body is an instrument, not just a vehicle to experience this reality through the senses, but also multidimensionally through feelings, intuition, thought and the Mind's Eye. The body is a complex, advanced instrument and we still don't understand the full mechanics and operation of it, even as we vibrate in harmony with the physical reality that determines our experience.

Get in the Water

As discussed earlier, water can be a great way to reset and clear any negative energy in your physical body, as well as your Light Body.

Once I had a conversation with a priest who said that even looping a hose like a lasso, and running water through it, then sliding it from head to toe over a person standing up, is good enough to remove negative energies, entities, and other undesirable influences.

Getting into the elements and currents of a river or the ocean with the salt and waves can do you a world of good. Dunk your head in the water and jump up and down and splash around. Even if you only do it for thirty seconds, water can do you a world of good. Of course, only swim under safe conditions and with supervision, if necessary.

You can clear your Light Body and energy in the shower by using your imagination and visualizing with the intent to clear. As you breathe out, imagine any negative energies or influences are leaving as the water runs over you. This might appear as black smoke or mist as it is leaving. Then, when you breathe in, visualize pure white light and Source energy coming into you.

Repeat this until you feel all negative energy is gone from within you, and then recycle positive white light energy as you breathe in and out for as long as it feels right. Finally, do a Clearing.

The Void Meditation

For this meditation, first do a Clearing as you sit in the blackness. Be aware that you are aware. Keep your eyes closed. Your intention is go to a place beyond the physical world by connecting to the world within.

Sensations of love and bliss might come through. You might cry and release emotions and negativity for yourself or others, even for the collective. By sensing the space around and within you as you sit in total darkness, this technique can be a conduit to take you beyond the physical dimension and into Source – the field where all emanates from. Joe Dispenza does amazing work with a similar type of meditation and I recommend looking at his material.

Love Light Bliss Mantra

This mantra meditation came to me spontaneously and I have continued to do it, on occasion. Simply repeat silently in your mind (or out loud) the words "love light bliss."

You can also repeat "love, light, bliss" with each inward breath. After the tension in your body and mind has been released, also try repeating it as you breathe out. This relaxing meditation can be done for as long as it feels right.

Simple Zen Meditation Practice

At times, it's good to get back to basics with this simple Zen meditation.

Sit up straight with your eyes open slightly and gaze at the floor in front of you. Now count to ten.

Count one on the in-breath, two on the out-breath, three on the in-breath, etc. If your mind wanders, go back and start at one again. Doing this simple exercise for five minutes can help you center yourself.

Chapter 8
WITNESS AWARENESS

Through meditation and the other practices discussed in this book it is possible to attain witness awareness. In this state, we are able to step out of our normal consciousness and into a broader consciousness in which we *witness* our experiences. In this state there is no judgment or criticism of ourselves or others. We are neutral in our awareness of self. The great Masters, yogis, and gurus exist in this state of consciousness.

Stories of old about Masters levitating, flying, bi-locating, manifesting various objects, and even creating intelligences might seem like fairy tales, but these things are real. We have heard stories about great yogis, lamas, sages, and seers. And in the words of Yeshua, "I have said, ye are gods; and all of you are children of the most High." Psalm 82:6, and, ""Verily, verily, I say unto you, He that believeth on me, the works that I do shall he do also; and greater works than these shall he do; because I go unto my Father." John 14:12

With these teachings, Yeshua was letting us know that what he could do, we can do also.

The Rainbow Body

Knowledge of the Rainbow Body comes from Tibet. Apparently, there are 160,000 documented cases of people who have achieved the Rainbow Body. This is a form of Ascension wherein a human being sheds the physical body and turns into light. This light is part of our true nature and it appears as a body made of a rainbow of colors.

This level of Ascension can be achieved through various practices, including meditation in a cave, doing tantric practices intensely for many years, including doing mudras, (particular movements of the hands) and speaking or chanting mantras. Other practices include manipulating the body in certain ways to activate the energetic body. Some don't achieve the Rainbow Body until they are dying and about to leave this world. Some do it in a shorter amount of time with years of dedication.

An example of this process is described as the body dissolving, leaving only hair and nails in a pile (or nothing at all) when the body turns into rainbow light. Sometimes rainbows appear in and around the building where the person is located at the time, and after the Rainbow Body has manifested. Alternatively, the physical body is left behind but it shrinks until it's the size of a large baby or small child with smooth skin. Then the rainbow light is seen around the general environment.

Another example of the Rainbow Body is when Yeshua came out of the tomb as a resurrected Being and there was a bright glow around him. Other possible evidence of this is the example of the shroud he was wrapped in while he was in the tomb. An imprint of his body appeared mysteriously on the shroud. It's theorized by some that when he left his physical form and became light, the ignition of the Light Body flash when turning into photon light left a negative image on the shroud, much like a photo negative. This burial shroud is known as *The Shroud of Turin*. It has been preserved in the Cathedral of Turin in Northern Italy since 1578 and has been studied repeatedly.

Padmasambhava was said to have bought the Rainbow Body Ascension teachings to Earth. He is known as the *Second Buddha*. Some believe he is an extraterrestrial who came to Earth in a lotus; some say he came in an egg. I have seen these types of crafts, been in them, and filmed them.

Padmasambhava was able to leave hand and footprints in stone and some say he was in India for over a thousand years before he brought his teachings to Tibet. It is said that all his disciples achieved the Rainbow Body through Dzogchen, which is the practice of achieving the *perfection* body. It is also said that the Rainbow Body teachings have been taught in thirteen star systems.

I experienced my own confirmation of this through interactions with a Being called *Ho-To* from Orion, who first appeared as a physical human with some slightly different features. When I was comfortable with it, Ho-To turned into a Rainbow Light Being. Then I found out many such Beings exist in the same location, which is a beautiful rainforest-like environment.

Ascension comes in many forms, including the advanced stages of the Rainbow Body, igniting your Merkabah/Light Body Vehicle, going to the New Earth, and raising your consciousness and entering a higher vibration in which you experience the many mansions. Just being a good person can help raise your frequency, which needs to be done before reaching for the advanced levels. This comes down to being a joyful, happy, compassionate, and loving human being, and using personal trauma as a vehicle to transcend the wrongs done to you and others.

Again, the "D" word, discipline, needs to be mentioned here, as this is what it takes to excel in the spiritual evolutionary process. As we rise to the occasion, abilities and experiences will unfold from within and into the outer and other worlds when we have been made ready through the preparation of the deep inner work.

With The Ascension and even the Rainbow Body and Merkabah practices, the negative you have experienced is used to drive you towards perfection. Some don't know this, but most of the consciously advanced extraterrestrials are still on the Ascension path. Even Light Beings are in the next stages of learning how to navigate the cosmos and going beyond light to a wave function. Next comes learning how to harmonize with Source, and then the opportunity to become a Creator Being yourself. At this point, we divide off from this universe (if you wish to do so) and create your own universe and realms within it. This, in turn, becomes a cell within the body of a greater intelligence that encompasses all Universes, Gods, and Creator Beings.

We can tap into this greater life force and our greater reality by observing and paying attention to whatever we sense and experience. This is simple, but it can lead to profound effects if understood and practiced regularly.

Vipassana Retreat

Once when doing a ten-day Vipassana meditation retreat, the place and space allowed for many things to be experienced. "Vipassana" means to see things as they really are. It's a type of meditation/teaching said by some to be the purest form of Buddhist teachings. It greatly enhances mindfulness. I see it as a stepping stone, a chapter in the *book of self-mastery*, not the end all be all, but well worth a try.

Before doing the retreat I meditated regularly. I was also doing remote viewing eight to twelve hours a day for three and a half years straight. Remote viewing is a psychic skill that involves viewing places, people, and situations at a distance. It's an advanced method of attaining impressions and visuals of something that actually exists in the physical dimension.

During some of this time, I still managed to work four hours a day at an accountancy firm and did a business management certificate, as well as other odd jobs.

In addition, I practiced Zen meditation, Pranayama, and the basics of yoga and Qigong. I wasn't a Master, but I was somewhat advanced due to being disciplined.

As I rose to the occasion down the path I am still on today in the human body on Earth, I was assisted by the Elohim, Shi-Ji from the Pleiades, Penkay from Orion, and Patama from Sirius, as well as other intelligences I later learned were old friends, and in some cases other aspects from the same Godhead. Going into the retreat, I saw it as a place to just *be* without distraction. After the introductory evening, there was to be no interaction with the outside world, no eye contact, and no phones or electronics, except when watching a video of the teacher Satya Narayana Goenka for an hour or so every night. It was perfect; just what I was looking for.

During the first evening meditation, my body started to vibrate, with some parts vibrating more intensely than others. I started to follow the vibration around until my whole body was vibrating.

We basically meditated from the early hours of the morning until late at night, and every few hours we were given meals and breaks.

At times, while in deep meditation, I would open my eyes and see golden orbs chasing dark masses out of the room. These dark, smoky, shadow masses looked like they were coming out of people and sometimes golden light would go into them. So, it seemed that during the retreat a form of Clearing and healing was going on.

One day while I was meditating, I felt an electrical-like shock from my root chakra go up my spine and out my crown chakra at the top of my head. This produced an incredible feeling of freeness, a lightness, and I opened my eyes.

Looking down, I realized I was levitating about three inches off the floor! But as soon as I realized consciously what was happening, my body dropped back down to the floor. In awe, shocked and stunned, I didn't know what to do or say, especially since no talking was allowed.

After calming down, I went back into meditation. But after some time had passed, it happened again!

Later I spoke to the teacher (if needed, this is allowed) and he said my karma was being released and a rebirth process was taking place. I took this on board and remained open-minded.

It seemed I was ahead of the other retreat participants, but I hadn't known it until the practices advanced and I realized I had already been doing them from day one. I didn't mind. It was about the inner work and releasing old patterns if they came up, going within, and being the observer. The apparitions and orbs kept things interesting while I was walking around the grounds and when I went to the bathroom and the place I was staying.

One day there was a massive thunderstorm and a double rainbow appeared in the sky in one direction, while in another direction there was a cigar-shaped extraterrestrial craft with many other scout ships around it. This was one time when I wished I had my camera so I could share footage of the crafts with the world, but it wasn't meant to be. I tried to make eye contact with the other students and I pointed up to the sky, but everyone was in their own zone. I laughed about this afterwards; it was just one of those things.

The point is that we each open up in our own way. I was already experiencing things like this on a regular basis through observation of my breathing, which is a big thing with Vipassana. It can also open you up to the reality that we are constantly vibrating. Given that we are being bombarded by the outside world via our senses, we don't have time to realize our inner experience.

When all you have to do over a matter of days is observe your breath, as simple as it sounds, discipline comes into play. Dharma is also a big part of the Vipassana teachings. It's a way of living with truth and following the righteous path of "do no harm."

As we were leaving the retreat, the teacher warned us it might take a few days to re-adjust to being in the world again after being in silence for so long and experiencing what we had. He was right.

After the Retreat

After leaving the retreat, it did take time to adjust, even with the number of practices I had been doing beforehand. I was already on the path of self-mastery by practicing meditation and remote viewing, and my otherworldly contacts with Shi-Ji and the Elohim. It was only the start of the journey I am still on.

Sometime later when driving home with a friend from the retreat, I remember him saying, "Do you feel that?" I said, "Yeah, there is a triangular craft overhead with a reptilian in it overlapping the car with negative intent." He said he could see it in his Mind's Eye and feel it, too. After going into clearing mode, soon enough it went its own way.

Next was a stop at a supermarket to meet family and friends, and get a razor and a few other things. Walking into the supermarket at the mall, I was taken aback by the number of signs about products and prices posted everywhere, no more than usual, but I realized how much it bombarded my heightened senses. It was a lot to take in after the retreat.

When I got to the shelves where the razors and shaving cream were I was overwhelmed by the number of choices. All I wanted was a razor, but there were so many to choose from. I stood in front the shelves trying to focus and find the product I wanted. The teacher was right; it was going to take time to adjust. But as it turned out, it didn't take as long as I thought it would. I was used to doing intense practices and I was also working and engaged in the daily activities of life before I did the retreat.

Now I carry Vipassana with me. To keep what you learn during a retreat like this, it is recommended that students meditate at least one hour a day. Like I said, this wasn't an issue for me; Vipassana is a stepping stone and well worth a try. Some of the retreat participants left days into it, due to the level of inner work that comes with it, including delving into the past, the mistakes they might have made, and the mental gymnastics.

Just like choosing shaving cream and razors at a supermarket, to have so many choices in this world is great, but when the number of choices is too much … well the point is how we react, how we behave, and what path we choose to take.

To have a choice is a beautiful thing, but some people do not have choices, or so it seems. Often, we are so bombarded by the external world that the purest experiences go unnoticed. As the familiar saying goes, "The best things in life are free."

Remote Viewing

I am well-practiced in being the observer, especially with touch sensation. When I went to the retreat, I was already using my observation abilities naturally to enter into witness awareness as a tool for multidimensional mind because of the amount of remote viewing I was doing at the time. In addition, I was doing regular meditation as relayed to me by Shi-Ji.

It was very interesting getting to know people who have worked for alphabet agencies in the U.S. and around the world, and professionally doing remote viewing, and through my travels and friendships. Project Stargate was a government-funded remote viewing program that was declassified in the 1990s. After that, remote viewing projects went to think tanks and private groups being hired for remote viewing projects, basically by governments, corporations, and the like. Projects involving targets to be viewed were outsourced and remote viewers went to working more with touch, sensation, and feeling.

Remote viewing was and is a tool to derive information by psychic means, and naturally, I was already doing it. Over time, my abilities and interactions developed and became more in-depth.

Now when I "view" a situation or Being, not only do I see it with my physical eyes or sense it non-physically, I also see flashes of imagery in my Mind's Eye. Even if my physical eyes are open, I receive thoughts with the flashes of vision and also emotions/feelings and sensations from each Being, along with informational downloads and/or thought forms. To communicate back, I project a thought about what I want to communicate.

More information on how to communicate with Spirit Guides, ETs and initiating contact can be found in my books *Connect to your Spirit and ET Guides* and *CE-5 Initiating Contact with Extraterrestrials*.

I remember walking into a remote viewing session led by John Vivanco. He was teaching at the ECETI ranch in Washington State in the U.S. at Master James Gilliland's ranch. John was upfront smiling as he looked at each student. A few of his colleagues were doing the course for practice as well and they were working on a target. John's focus in this practice was basically to get them to *feel* the target to know what it was. When I walked up to him and said "dolphin," he simply shook his head and smiled.

The students had their eyes closed and their hands by their sides as they stood and made movements like a dolphin. It was funny and would have seemed crazy if you didn't know you were in a class learning remote viewing.

It's amazing to see how most newcomers to this practice are innocent and get the targets straight away – not everyone, but everyone and anyone can remote view.

There are periods starting out when your abilities can dip down, but if you stick with it, you will end up learning how to remote view. Like anything, practice makes perfect, but it also comes down to the "D" word again, discipline.

There is much that goes unseen. The human eye can only perceive a fraction of 0.005 of the electromagnetic spectrum which is visible light.

Many intelligences are not just extraterrestrials living out in space, but some are here on Earth, maybe even standing right next to you. This might include ultra-terrestrials, nature spirits, or thought forms; even inside the Earth there are pockets of intelligences. Gaia and the Sun are intelligent, too.

Vibration is a by-product of being in the presence of another intelligence, but you might not recognize it unless you are acquainted with sensation/vibration, thoughts, and temperature changes in terms of how these experiences relate to contact with other intelligences in this reality or elsewhere. Much can go unnoticed unless you have a natural talent for picking up on these things. With communication via telepathy being a daily thing for me – and at times old friends and family from other worlds materializing in my presence and/or visiting in their ships – each contact amplifies my senses. This would be the case for those who have their own inner contact.

Walking the street in a city or being in an old town much I can see, whether it's from another time or what resides just outside of what we call our normal reality.

Beechworth is an example. This old gold rush town is located in Victoria Australia. Partly known for its gold and the famous bushranger Ned Kelly, as well as its bakery, Beechworth is rich in historic culture. Unfortunately, many Chinese people were killed there for their gold during the gold rush. They had come to Beechworth in hopes of striking it rich and making a life for themselves. However, even further back in time the Original People had lived and died in the area. This is a sad history, but it has also enriched the land with energy. This area is so haunted that many sensitives don't mind the town, but they are guarded naturally without knowing the place or its history.

Spirits from the other side and even existing in other times overlap this reality and live among us in the present. Especially in areas like Beechworth, which offers popular ghost tours. It can be confusing to some if they don't know they are seeing what some would say are spirits of the dead, but they are very much alive, just existing in another state of energy/consciousness/awareness.

It's the same for me in a city like Melbourne. For example, walking the streets I see apparitions of intelligence, both human and non-human, walking among the population. Even though I was young when this started, I thought it was normal and that everyone could see them. I had to shut down and keep this awareness in the background for many years. Later, I began to understand what I was seeing and that most people don't see what I see. I embraced it and began to use it to assist others with messages, or I would help those in other frequencies move on to their perfect place in the universe.

Communicating with Other Intelligences

I went to Bali once and traveled the many temples and sacred sites there. Such a beautiful country. Although many see it as a poor third world country, the nature and smile of the Balinese people are some of the biggest and most heartfelt I have ever seen.

They are a simple people with simple needs. They burn incense outside of their temples, shops, and homes and some greet you with, "Om Swastiastu," which means, "May the Gods bless you," It's such a beautiful saying, and I began to use it myself.

Staying in Ubud one day inland, I awoke to the sounds of nature and took a trip to the Valley of the Kings (Gunung Kawi). In the valley, I visited an eleventh century temple and then the Elephant Temple (Goa Gajah), a ninth century temple. More than this was covered during the trip, but these were significant, as will be explained.

At the Valley of the Kings, walking down the many steps there (let me say, many, many steps) I came to a spot where the sides of the valley were carved out and majestic temples had been carved into the sides of the valley. Doors and windows, which would normally be outside structures, were carved into the rock. It was incredible and amazing.

The doors and outer structures carved into the rock don't actually open, and most would think it is all for show. But I can tell you for sure they are doors to other dimensions. Some of these doors and windows can take you to another world overlapping ours in another frequency, and also to other worlds.

At the entrance at the bottom of the steps, after crossing a type of bridge, I was approached by a few White Light Beings. This was unseen by the people around me, but I could tell they felt the presence of the Beings because they reacted by having goose bumps.

It was revealed to me through telepathic communication that the area and structures are a lot older than what is publicly known or stated, and that the area was and is a meeting place that houses a council conglomerate from Lemuria and Atlantis. You could say the enlightened from that former time are near this area, and there is also a Hall of Records, one of three in different places on

Self Mastery – The Path to Ascension

Earth. And let me say, the Beings are there right now but they go unseen or felt by most of the population, including locals and visitors from afar.

An energy and vibration went throughout my body to the point I was almost in tears from the bliss and had to sit down, not just from being in the presence of the White Light Beings, but due to the download of information they transmitted about the area's history, what they are, and why they are there.

There are reasons why I cannot mention everything about my experience with these Beings except what I have, because of the personal and intimate nature of the information. But I have shared what I can.

You see, over time, I have come to understand our experiences are about us, individually. I say this not out of ego, but because that's how it is. However, the fruit from our experiences paves the way for us to understand our place in the collective and how, through this, everything is tailored for everyone to play their part in and for the collective.

Everyone has a path, a journey, and each is as important as the next person's. We are all part of a massive jigsaw puzzle and each person's journey has an equal effect on another's.

Next I visited the Elephant Temple, which was also quite amazing. There were many people and tourists, so I waited to enter the temple. When my turn came and I walked in, I saw carved-out spots, about waist high, and inside each one I could see the same types of Beings as in the Valley of the Kings. Yes, there were White Light Beings just sitting inside each carved-out spot. They looked like they were meditating. It also seemed like they are part of the mechanics of the area in a multidimensional way.

I was taken aback but continued down a walkway. And In each spot there was a Light Being where the wall was carved out. They picked up on my presence and vice-versa. Taking a moment to allow for permission to be there and to see and interact with them, I gave thanks and went on my way.

Nearby on the Island of Java, an ancient pyramid (or maybe pyramids) was uncovered in recent years. During the communications I received at the Valley of the Kings, I already knew this area has one Hall of Records. Other communications in the past have said there is another one underground in the area of the Sphinx in Egypt, and the third is somewhere in the area of Bermuda. The Hall of Records is believed to contain a complete record of everything that has happened in all time, including records of each soul's history and actions.

Only time will tell, but the heart can by-pass the need for these physical locations of light information, which can be tapped into. The singularity point we come from and go back to, a point from which all is projected and emanates from.

No matter where you are, you might feel goose bumps, temperature changes, hair standing up, a feeling of not being alone, and energy sensations as a by-product of another intelligence, a Light Body overlapping yours.

If you are going into a meditative state when this happens, first do a Clearing and then project questions by thought. Observe your emotions, feelings, visions, ideas, and knowingness. The unusual sensations could mean communications are coming back to you from another intelligence. On an intuitive level, it's almost like talking to yourself in your mind.

A word or idea is a response, equivalent to a chapter heading. Minutes, hours, a day later, a knowingness of more information might come through. This is the rest of the information integrating from the Light Body into your human mind as it is being diluted down into a digestible manner.

On an even more out there level, with regard to contact and communication, sometimes, an intelligence such as an extraterrestrial might land a craft on you, just outside the frequency of our reality, and/or vibrate you on board physically or your energy body, or even communicate through visions and telepathy. A ghost or other apparition can communicate in the same way.

When talking to elders of the original people in Australia and native people in America, I was told this phenomenon was known by them. In other words, people on both sides of the world were surprised when I talked about this because it was something they knew but did not really speak about.

I have spent a bit of time with the King of the Raven Tribe, Uluki Brendan Murray, here in Australia and been initiated into the Raven Tribe. Through our talks, the ancients have shared much, and much of it coincides with the Native Americans, especially through meeting Zuni Pueblo Indian elder Clifford Mahooty. He is with us in spirit now, but when he was alive he was a member of the tribal orders of the Kachina Priesthood, the Galaxy Medicine Society, the Sun Clan, and Wisdom Keeper of the Zuni history and their spiritual practices.

Many ties in together from my own experience and what the Original people in Australia and Native Americans have to say, as well as a couple of former theologians for the Pope, whom I have met with.

Vibration, energy sensation, hair standing up, temperature changes, and a feeling of not being alone – these things can happen anywhere at any time. In some cases they are signs another intelligence is nearby.

These sensations might also be present when a healing takes place, or when you are in a vortex portal site and/or ancient locations where not just Beings still reside, but where information can be stored ethereally in a location, or even in a rock. Information can be downloaded and transmitted to human consciousness in these places. A sensation can also accompany this when going into a state of multidimensional mind. In this state it is possible to experience the many mansions, *i.e.*, realms in God's Mind, and see the fractal kaleidoscope geometric nature outside of Source's true state, in which intelligences can bleed in and out of the transmissions within Source. This place I call the *geometric light realms* and/or the *Angelic kingdom*. Observation and witnessing yourself being the observer are key for this to unfold.

Also important is understanding our reality and realms of vibration. Let's say, as an analogy, we vibrate at one frequency and another intelligence is overlapping our reality at another frequency. At times, they might appear in physical form, or they might appear as an apparition and bleed in and out of our reality, or vice versa, depending on how you look at it. The place of awareness and feeling is one in which we can communicate, because even if the person or Being is outside of our full visual view, we are still in each other's presence.

Imagine the ether is God and your Mind's Eye is a television. You can't see the television waves being broadcast, but if you turn on your TV and tune into a channel, a program comes on that you can observe and witness. Earth reality is a program, one of many.

Encounters with Bigfoot

Our big hairy friend Bigfoot is seen phasing in and out regularly, sometimes with crafts or orbs of light. Yes, Bigfoot is real; in two countries I have seen three species. From experience and the knowledge I possess about them, I can say some reside locally, some are extraterrestrial in nature, and yes, they have multidimensional abilities but the level of their abilities depends on the individual.

Once when I was in Queensland Australia on a property in a portal area, I felt a strange sensation come over me. Suddenly, I experienced a red overlay with our reality; it was like red cellophane was over my eyes and I saw a Bigfoot. Extremely tall it was, with a big build and no neck (or so it seemed). Its hair was dark brown and short with what looked like dreadlocks, almost like twigs all over it. The creature had red eyes. This vision only lasted for about 10 seconds and then everything went back to what we think of as "normal."

An example of seeing Bigfoot phasing out physically occurred when I was at ECETI Ranch in Washington State in the U.S. ECETI is a spiritual mecca, of sorts, and home to James Gilliland. Near the end of my mid-morning walk, as I was going back towards James's cabin, I saw a Bigfoot about 6 feet tall (not a big one). It had mixed grey, dark, and light brown hair about half a foot long all over it, and it walked like Shaggy from Scooby Doo.

I watched it walk about fifteen feet, give or take, and then it just phased out. Just at that moment, James opened the door to his cabin and came out. He saw me about fifty feet away just frozen and asked what had happened. He could tell *something* unusual was going on from the way I was just standing there, I told him a Bigfoot just walked between his place and where I was standing.

This is a common occurrence at ECETI, along with the Masters and ET visitors. The many Bigfoot sightings and foot casts of Bigfoot add to the rich history of the beautiful area in southeast Washington. (See: www.eceti.org.)

Our human history is much stranger than most of us realize, and I don't mean just going off-world but the multidimensional nature of it, too.

Exercises – Tips and Tools

Observation/Sensation Exercise

This exercise is very simple, but don't do it if it feels like a chore.

1. First, blindfold yourself and either put in earplugs or turn on a fan to create white noise, or do nothing at all.

2. Then lay down (or sit up if you prefer) and do a Clearing.

3. Witness yourself observing from the inner place in which you are aware you are aware. Observe any noises, visions, thoughts, or sensations for five minutes.

I do this exercise from forty minutes to an hour a day, five days a week because it's helpful for exercising the senses and raising awareness.

It also allows for insight and experiences to take place, if you first set your intention to experience something insightful and/or guidance on how to be the best version of yourself, be of service, and/or bring more love and joy into your life. From this place, just be. What needs to happen will happen, if anything at all.

Water and Food

Many people go without water and food, although a lot are lucky in some parts of the world to have an abundance of both. Many wish they had more, while many with more take it for granted.

Give or take, seventy percent of our body is made up of water. If you are not drinking enough water, try to drink *at least* one glass every morning, noon, and at dinner. Being adequately hydrated will help you think clearly and function smoothly. If you can, try to drink alkaline water, which is beneficial for healing and water absorption. There are many different diets, including vegetarian, vegan, paleo, and meat, plus other categories. I don't tell anyone what they should do with regard to food; only you can decide what's best. However, I believe eating healthy, organic food grown close to the Earth without preservatives, hormones, antibiotics, and the like is the best way to nourish yourself. Also try to eat some fruit and vegetables every day.

Organically grown raw foods are high-energy because they are uncooked and they have been raised naturally. They provide great fuel, but unless you have adopted a raw food diet, it's hard to explain.

Whole, raw food assists with the mind/body/spirit connection, including connection with the Light Body. I also recommend green superfood powders, which are great in assisting with all dietary needs and detoxing at the same time.

I have smoothies made with bananas, blueberries, nuts, water, plant protein, and green superfood powder twice a day. I also have hummus and corn chips. This is basically my diet, but do whatever floats your boat and keeps you healthy.

I also recommend Intermittent fasting, even at the basic level of not eating after the sun goes down. This dietary practice can be very effective in keeping you strong with good energy, your weight down, and helping with digestion and stomach health.

Bless Your Food and Water

As seen with Dr. Emoto's work, thoughts affect water. This has been verified by exposing water to words, intentions, and prayer, and then freezing it. For example, you can see the beautiful geometric structure of the frozen water droplets after being exposed to positive words like "love" and "happy." Each word produces a different and unique effect of beautiful snowflake-like geometry on each frozen droplet. Likewise, when water is exposed to words such as "hate" and "fear," there are no beautiful geometric patterns, only distorted randomly structured ice.

Geometry is found in nature all around us. When there is harmony, there is geometry, even in the blueprint of our reality, where all is structured from light and has a geometric blueprint. Working with a positive mind and intention creates a blueprint which can be joyous. When working from the light blueprint, you can create and manifest. Something as simple as a prayer or Clearing goes throughout the molecular structure of the body, and remember, we are mostly water, so think about how much a prayer or sending positive thoughts of love and gratitude to the water you drink and the food you eat can be.

Self-Inquiry

Some might think self-inquiry means just spending time alone. However, by focusing on the present moment during the practice of self-inquiry, self-realization comes into play. Patterns, problems, insights, and answers can arise, along with opportunities, when working from an optimistic and unbounded positive mind and seeing all possibilities.

Answers and resolutions come, naturally, but sitting and being in the self-inquiry state are key to self-mastery. Likewise, the realization that you are a manifestation of Source is important. You are a Creator Being yourself, capable of manifesting. Your mind is your servant and your body is, too.

To practice self-inquiry, sit for five minutes, empty your mind, and just be. Do this regularly, even if only once a day. During this time, you will discover resolutions, answers, ideas, and insights that might surprise you. All your questions can be answered in the present moment, in silence.

Connecting to Nature

Our human nature is multidimensional and many other intelligences and Beings exist right beside us, although they are unseen by most. Worlds and dimensions overlap and each realm affects another. Gaia is alive and the elements are, too. Everything is part of this realm's makeup. Intelligences, local and non-local, and Guardians exist all over the planets, satellites, stars, and vortex portal sites. Ask for permission when you're in the mountains, by rivers and streams, and the beautiful rainforests, deserts, and/or ancient locations and sites. Set the intention for why you're there, whether it's to go for a walk, connect to spirit, and/or communicate with the trees, animals, elementals, or fairies, and even rocks. Who knows, Bigfoot might show up!

Always ask for permission to be in nature, give thanks, and set an intention. In this simple way you can show your respect and create safety in the experience.

Working with Original Elders in Australia, a common thing for ancient places (and something that becomes second nature) is using intuition and intention with regard to a tree or rock at an entry point to a location or at the site. Most of the time they blend in, but they also stand out in terms of the size and/or energy the tree or rock gives off.

Sometimes, the biggest, fattest, tallest tree in the area is a good place to ask for permission. Usually there is a feminine or masculine tree at a site, and this can also be a good place to ask for permission to be in the area. Some trees are so big that even when giving them a hug you cannot get your arms a quarter of the way around them; likewise, some rocks are gigantic. There's a feeling of nature talking to you when your intuition kicks in. This will let you know what to connect to and communicate with. Trees and rocks are conscious, and they can be a focal point in communicating with all other life in the area. How would you feel if someone you've never met just walked into your home? It's the same with all life in its natural environment.

The next time you are out in nature, try to identify which tree or rock to touch and speak to. Do this intuitively or vocally. Sometimes even the rocks can download and communicate ancient knowledge or information left by another or that might be stored in the area. So be aware of your thoughts, feelings, and visions.

In some places you might be guided to be cleansed before going any further. Again, use your intuition. This might mean taking a blend of leaves from surrounding plants and burning them in the bark from a tree, although again this is an intuitive thing that is usually done at sacred sites. Even sage can be used in some cases. Just don't cause a fire. As superstitious as some of this might sound, I know from experience these things can affect you in some locations.

Show respect to build a relationship with the intelligences in certain areas, including ancestor spirits, the Guardians, nature spirits, and the living plants, trees, and rocks.

Basically, when entering or already at a site, stop and look around. Is a specific tree or rock speaking to you; does anything else stand out? If so, walk up to it, put your hand on it, ask for permission, and speak your intention. You will know intuitively if it's okay to enter and spend time there. Most often, your respect will be appreciated by the local intelligence(s).

Sometimes, like sites here in Australia, there are female and male areas. Sometimes this is a strict thing, but other times it's flexible. For example, let's say a man is with a female in a female area, it's okay. It's always best to ask the Original People about the protocols when visiting ancient sites. You will be appreciated for your respect and likely granted permission.

Chapter 9
MULTIDIMENSIONAL VISION

Made of rhombohedron calcite crystals, the pineal gland when compressed gives off a piezoelectric effect. This is a scientific fact we know about the pineal gland today.

What you can't prove (although in my opinion it's true) is that when the piezoelectric effect takes place, in effect, it turns on the ability of the pineal gland associated with the Mind's Eye, *i.e.,* clairvoyance. This important gland is located in the center of the brain, and it's associated with the Sixth Chakra in the energy body.

The pineal gland is a biological device that taps you into the Light Body. The Light Body overlaps the physical body and it's able to interface with all realms of existence. When your intention is focused on a frequency, you become a vibrational match for that realm, intelligence, or even your Higher Self and Source. You will get visuals and communication – not just visuals, but also information through thoughts, feelings, and emotions, which can also bring awareness and information, as well as through the five senses, including sight, sound, touch, taste, and smell.

The pineal gland is responsible for producing melatonin in the body. It also enables multidimensional visions and experiences because of a process the melatonin goes through, eventually producing DMT (dimethyltryptamine). This is also produced in plants and animals, and humans sometimes take it contained within some psychedelic drugs.

These days DMT is being used for spiritual and healing purposes, but it should not be abused, and it needs to be taken under the supervision of a Shaman. In some cases, it is being used in various forms in medical settings, although it is illegal in most places.

Plant medicines such as peyote, magic mushrooms, and the poison from a toad (as Mike Tyson would say; he has taken it"), are being used in many places. These plant medicines are not always taken for the right reasons, and they can be a shortcut for an experience. Yes, they might be useful for some people in opening the Mind's Eye to see beyond the veil, but don't forget that through intention and understanding the mechanics of the body, mind, and spirit connection the same experiences can be produced naturally. Also, taking these substances can bring down your psychic barriers, causing the gates to your psyche to open and allow negative influences to enter through the holes created in your aura. These things are not necessary to have an illuminating experience, and in my opinion, it is best to make the effort to do spiritual practices and produce these experiences naturally.

Ancient cultures knew this, and that is why they used mantras, danced for long periods of time, worked with the chakras, and yes, some spoke to the plants and knew how to create substances for journeying. There are many ways to go multidimensional, but DMT is produced naturally when we sleep. If you get to know your own mechanics, the dream and inner vision state will come through coherently, clearly, and safely.

Synchronicities

You will come across many intelligences (Beings) as you reach for Ascension, both seen and unseen, and there will be signs showing the way. This can be quite simple. For example, two people who have never met might bring up the same topic in casual conversation. Perhaps you are walking down the street one day and you begin to think of someone you haven't seen in years. You turn a corner and suddenly that person is walking towards you. Someone comes to mind and in that moment the phone rings and it's that same person. Perhaps you have been wanting to buy a used car, a specific older model. Again you are walking down the street and when you turn a corner right before you is that very same car with a For Sale sign on it. These types of events are called *synchronicities*.

Once I was on a plane going to Rome. It was my first time going to that part of the world; previously, the furthest I had been northwest of Australia was when I went to Bali. It was exciting to be flying to Europe. During the flight, I wasn't sure which countries we would be flying over. Then all of a sudden, some time into the flight the pilot spoke over the intercom and said, "To our right, are the Pyramids." I was surprised to realize we were flying over Egypt. At that moment I was looking at the map on the screen on the back of the headrests. The clock said it was 11:11.

Other times, I might be thinking about a decision, a person, or a project, and again, another triple or quadruple number would appear on a clock or car number plate. Some people think of this phenomenon as *Angel Numbers*. This is just one of many names given for this phenomenon. Some people go on-line to Google for more information about Angel Numbers. Yes, you can do this, but also take notice of what's occurring in your life at the time. What are you thinking about? What is your intuition telling you? Always follow your heart and inner knowing.

God, the universe, Angels, celestials, guides, extraterrestrials and more are waiting to assist us, and sometimes they connect through synchronicities to let us know we are on the right path.

Some people live by the numbers but, in truth, number synchronicities are just a heads up that tells us to keep doing what we are doing. Perhaps you had an idea to look at a clock, number plate, car dashboard, computer, phone, etc. and 444 appears, but *maybe* it's a thought projection from another intelligence. It's like someone suddenly getting an impulse to go outside and check if the car is locked, and when they go out, they see a UFO!

Ear ringing is also common, and sometimes it is related to Shift symptoms, the Schumann resonance, solar flares, and/or downloads. This is different from tinnitus, although most label it as such. It can also be that you are picking up on different energy frequencies. It might mean the Earth or Sun is going through something unusual that day. Gaia is a living intelligence and so is the sun. We harmonize with the Earth and the sun.

Sometimes the Earth and sun amplify our energies and it's up to us to rise to the occasion and embrace the change and heal, including releasing the past.

All is vibration; nature is vibration, and when we are in harmony and feeling good vibrations, everything comes together and can be amplified. Look at nature, from cicadas to frogs croaking in harmony, to the purr of a cat, which can be healing.

Our feelings are a vibration; our body is vibrating; and our Light Body is vibrating. The only time this does not apply is when you are in harmony with Source. As we develop our frequency and raise it, unlocking the dormant DNA is natural as it starts to come online in a process aligned with your development. Everything is all about frequency.

As humans we want validation; we want the truth, and so we should, but acceptance and validation outside of ourselves is a hurdle most face throughout most of their life. This, in turn, leads to living another's life, another's truth that is not our own, which can be bitter for the soul.

In my travels both on and off-world, I've learned that everyone wants to be happy. But we need to be responsible for our own happiness; it's not something that is given to us from an external source.

Whether from the Elohim state or off-world visitors, the times of Lyra, the reptilian custodianship, the Pleiadians custodian ship before the inception of Atlantis and Lemuria, and even now, many of you have been here a long time and come from other worlds, but you all originally came from Source.

There were times in the past when ancients in different pockets of the world evolved and ascended, and many are still in a higher evolutionary process in pockets inside the Earth, too. Places like Shambala exist outside the frequency we are currently able to perceive.

The point is we can direct our future *and* our today. Many say, "I am not coming back," and I can understand that, but the reasons why you are here, what you are doing here, and who you truly are come at a time when resistance is released. Being open to all possibilities opens you up without filters and programming in the search for truth.

We are constantly going through transformational cycles. This life is but a transformation, and death is but a transformation. From the cocoon to the butterfly, fly you will.

The basics are all you need. You are not your emotions, thoughts, and feelings; you are witnessing them, and depending on your willpower, determination, and discipline is how you will operate and experience your life. You are the driver; you are not the car, but you can be both and operate in synch. Your trip can be smooth and safe when you are in control of your emotions. At times, it will be bumpy, but those times are lessons, not mistakes, unless you don't take notice of the signs when they present themselves. Mastery is a path for all, and if at times it seems lonely, know you are never alone.

Be the light in the darkness, be the love, joy, and bliss in the storm, a light to others, and when the time is right the Sun of Source will present itself. And it will be a reunion on a grand scale. Ascension

Self Mastery – The Path to Ascension

awaits you, and so does what lies behind and beyond Ascension. This is a whole new journey.

All paths are different avenues to Source, and self-mastery is fundamental to all of them. Focus, determination, and being present will reveal clarity on the path. Some think initiations from a sage, Master, or guru will solve their problems and they will be enlightened, but true Masters assist other Masters, which is really what all this is all about. We are already Masters; we just need to find it in ourselves. Great responsibilities come with it, and initiations should only be done when a person has risen to the next stage in their evolutionary process.

Enlightenment can't be given. It is a right for all of us, but the inner work must be done first. This includes the higher level of service required as you go through the stages of self-mastery and inner development. Unless you go full Rainbow Body in your Ascension process, you are still going to have to brush your teeth and have a shower – if you also want good health and hygiene. Self-mastery means experiencing joy, whether you are in the eye of a storm or under the sun.

It's okay to cry, to feel, to hug, to touch, to love. These emotions are for you to experience. We carry our experiences with us. The highs, the lows, the ups and the downs – this is just a ride and you can't hide from your true nature. The before and after is where you will not find all knowledge. It is hidden in the present and it's a gift. Find yourself – it's what you have been waiting for.

The Dreamtime

Dreaming is more than what most people think, and ignoring your dreams as having no substance is an injustice. Contact can happen in our dreams, as well as information from our Higher Self, Source, Spirit Guides, ETs, Masters, Angels, and the like, although sometimes the information is transmitted in the form of symbols. The word *dreamtime* comes from the Original people of Australia.

When we remember our dreams, sometimes they are multidimensional experiences and/or spirits, other Beings, or the Higher Self transmitting information to us symbolically while we are asleep. Even our intention for the Higher Self and Guides to communicate in our Dreamtime can be enough for insight with guidance to come through.

Most of these intelligences and Higher Beings see us as light and the blueprint of this reality. This makes it easier for them to come through vibrationally.

I do have to mention that sometimes what you see can be symbolic for what the higher state of your true nature is trying to tell or show you.

Coming back to the fact that we can only see a fraction of 0.005 percent of the electromagnetic spectrum – and that being the visible light spectrum – our brain has to decode multidimensional information. Basically, we see with our brain, our beliefs, or whatever we are open to. This why a few people might be together when an experience of a paranormal nature takes place, whether seeing a Being, an ET and/or a UFO, etc., and some see it and some don't.

In the case of the pineal gland/Third Eye, sometimes you might see something in a 3D type of way with your eyes open, or in a vision, but sometimes the brain has to decode the information symbolically from what the Light Body is experiencing in a higher state if the experience is beyond a 3D nature.

In this case, the brain must decode it in such a way that the information or vision might not be exactly what happened, but rather it's symbolic for what the intelligences you are interacting with from a higher realm, or the Higher Self, are trying to relay. In this case, through feeling and intuition you can decode the information coming through, once you become adapted to multidimensional mind.

Over time, through inner work and self-inquiry, you will work out the meaning and insight that is specific and unique to you. You will learn to see the synchronicities and even get information ahead of time through intuition and thoughts. These things are likely to happen on a regular basis through being open and on the spiritual path. You are "in the wind" with it, but don't worry; the revelations that are meant to come through will when the time is right.

Just like with past lives (even though everything is happening at the same time), if you knew everything at once, your human brain as it is now wouldn't be able to handle it, although if running at 100 percent maybe you could. The brain is like a hard drive on a computer; as more and more information goes into it, your memory can get too full and things need to be deleted so it can run smoothly again. In terms of the human mind and how it interacts with the Light Body, if you know everything, you can be distracted from the present. But, also, all information is accessible via Source, which can be compared to the "cloud" in today's technological terms.

Light, sound, and matter are illusionary, once you surpass all that and go into a wave function as the unbounded being you are. All is accessible at once and the mechanics I speak of here are obsolete when you are back to your true nature and all-knowing state.

Meditating in darkness and being blindfolded for periods during the day, in combination with your focus and intention, will enable visions to come through.

Some even believe that around 2:00 p.m. is when they are the most effective in terms of psychic abilities because of the sun's location during the day. You can decide what's best for you. The sun and the location of our planet in the solar system and where we are in the galaxy are factors in this timing. There are many factors, but in the end, multidimensional mind can unfold at any time.

Being the observer while also knowing that you are the observer and connecting to the part of you that is aware is key for the Third Eye to open and connecting to multidimensional mind.

A common practice is to get up between 2:00 and 3:00 a.m. and have a tea or coffee, meditate or read, and then go back to sleep. I have noticed that between 5:00 and 7:00 a.m. a multidimensional dream state experience can occur. This isn't like a normal dream in which you remember details when you first wake up and forget them soon afterwards. The practice I've outlined above could be considered a dream quest experience, which can be very helpful in soul development.

Also, it's best not to wear sunglasses too much during the day because natural light is nourishing for the physical eyes, and it also gives the pineal gland and the brain what they need to work more efficiently.

In some places around the world manmade toxicity from elements like fluoride cause calcification in the pineal gland and other health concerns. So take care to avoid toxic foods, drinks and chemicals. Your determination and strength to live a "clean" lifestyle can override any situation that arises.

Some people don't dream or they don't remember their dreams. When you don't dream, sometimes for long periods of time, out-of-body experiences might not bleed through to your human consciousness. Perhaps these multidimensional experiences are too overwhelming or they interfere with your life, or maybe not remembering them is a protection mechanism, because they might be too far out for you to integrate and comprehend. So, basically, don't worry if you are not having visionary dreams; they will come, in time.

Vibration is key for how spiritual evolution unfolds. As an example, if you are in a good mood, you match a higher frequency, and higher intelligences can come through. If you are in a negative state of mind, lower intelligences can come through. Always look at the fruit of your experience, especially your spiritual experiences. The knowledge that comes through is key, and not giving your power over to another is also key. Stand in your own power and authority because we are all equals in the universe of God's Mind.

We experience simulations within simulations in the Mind of God, but connecting to the higher unbounded state overrides all and connects you to all that is. In this state, Satya (truth) can be seen. This is all that matters. We all have different experiences and outlooks, whether we are male or female. Our identification in this world does not matter in the higher realms because sex, race, or religion is not an issue in the bigger picture, nor in God's Mind.

If we can get out of our own way and give up our preconceived notions and programming, and we make an effort, all is available to be experienced. There are no limits in the process of Ascension!

Letting go and being open to our true nature is key in the process of unlocking and reconnecting with the beautiful, wonderful, and loving nature of who we are and what we come from and are always connected to.

With this said, we do have to remember we are spirit having a human experience and embrace the beautiful nature of the experience. Often we get caught in the trap of worrying about what's not working. It comes down to balance, gratitude, and being grounded in our endeavors and pursuits. Joy and love are to be shared with others. You cannot be completely reclusive. Most introverts also have extroverted qualities and vice versa, depending on their environment and those they surround themselves with. So it's always best to follow the direction your soul pulls you towards.

The Joys of the Body

As simple as it sounds, many like to socialize with others but some don't do it. The human experience comes with the aspect of interaction, but as for the how and who, simply follow your bliss in making choices. The key is to remember everyone is a teacher and also a student. Like everything else in life, where your awareness lies, there also lies your experience.

Being around positive, uplifting, and loving people can be joyous, and it can even bring those who are not social out of their shells. Everyone has different points of view as to the nature of this reality. We see the world around us through our own lens in our own way. We are not all meant to be the same. We leave Source and incarnate in order to experience all possibilities, so enjoy the uniqueness and gifts, and don't forget to give as well as receive; the Earth experience is meant to be shared.

Sexual desire can divert your path with temptation if not done from a place of love. We are social beings and love is our true nature. Let your heart direct you; use it as your compass. When joining physically with a partner, consider visualizing your chakras and light bodies merging. Enjoy the journey, not for climaxing, but as a Tantric experience, one of many methods that are a lot deeper than explained here technique-wise and with safety protocols. A powerful energy experience can arise during tantric sex. Partners can also join their intentions for stronger manifestation and co-creating. Some people call this *sex magic*, a term that is not just connected to Egyptian times, but also to other cultures on and off-world.

Worth a mention here is being balanced in your masculine and feminine energies. This is vital for productivity and balance when the inner and outer worlds come into play in terms of your development. The masculine is assertive and structured, and gets stuff done. Whereas, the feminine is loving, nurturing, great for manifesting, thinking creatively, and is great for connecting to Source.

Who you share your energy with is important. This affects your mental, emotional and physical state and the Light Body. Love and sexuality are to be shared, and the respect, appreciation and experience that comes with making love is a glimmer of God's love, as well as the gifts that love can produce, including children and feelings of bliss.

Much pleasure can be had from a touch, a hug, or an embrace from another. The field of the heart is always interfacing with others who open their hearts to us. Have a laugh, go out to dinner, dance, sing, and be joyful. Dancing is an expression of your energy, of your love; it's a story, and it also has an effect on the energy bands of the body. Dancing can be of great benefit, just like art or writing, and it can be therapy, a way to express yourself. All these things are for us to enjoy!

Be grounded, be human. Yes, you are a Spiritual Being having a human experience, and you are here to learn, enjoy, and participate in uplifting humanity to its full potential. You are an expression of Source, a child of God, but you are also here for the human experience, a joyful experience with so much potential.

So, experience Source and God's love in the human experience. I'm sure God won't mind. Parents always like to see their children laugh, play, and have fun.

Exercises – Tips and Tools

Candlelight Meditation

Many want to open their Third Eye, but it's also about maintaining and exercising it for spiritual evolution. A very simple technique for this is the Candlelight Meditation:

First, light a candle in a lightly lit or dark room.

Stare at the candle for five seconds and then close your eyes and continue to see it in your imagination until the vision fades. As you continue to see it, even with your eyes closed, see it with intention. Your imagination includes all possibilities and is God's imagination.

Starting out, some might not see the candlelight with their eyes closed, while others will. Repeat this practice, even for a couple of minutes, and it will begin to enhance your capability to see with your Mind's Eye.

Om Meditation

The sinus cavity in the human body is hollow. Thus, the sounds we make create a vibration that can cause a piezoelectric effect in the pineal gland. In my experience, this opens and/or activates the pineal gland as the crystals in it vibrate.

Sitting for five minutes and repeating the Om mantra can help open and activate the pineal gland through the vibration. You can also try your own or another mantra.

Sit in a meditative pose and repeat "Om" as you breathe out. Continue as long as you want. Even two minutes can make a difference. This meditation can also be done as a slow chant.

Patience is needed because sometimes it takes a bit of time to open up the pineal gland and have visions. However, after it happens, the visions will continue to happen on and off periodically. Over time, this can be a regular thing, if desired.

Dancing

It doesn't matter what kind of music you like to dance to. And it doesn't matter if you dance alone in your room or you go to a club or dance class and dance with others. No matter how or where you dance, you will enjoy the free movement and energy found in dancing.

Music assists with uplifting our energies and breaks down and rebuilds the energy bands. The sound waves also assist with this, as well as dancing being good exercise for physical strengthening and coordination.

Everything in all universes and all dimensions is vibration, including music and dancing. The sound waves going through the body, the environment, the feeling, emotions and movement can change your mood. Happy music = happy dancing = happy life.

Making Art

If you are so inclined, making art is a good way to express yourself, a way to communicate, a way to vent and teach another, and it's good for the soul. There's so much art can communicate that words cannot.

Whether you choose drawing, painting, sculpture, or collage, the colors and the subject depicted will enrich your experience. Art can be food for thought and for the soul. Express yourself. You might choose to create something representing your spiritual experiences, as in an expression of your inner visions, insight, revelations, and perception. The art you create can also offer a vision of Source, The Creator, and multidimensional reality to others.

Write and/or Keep a Diary

Keeping a record of your experiences is highly recommended. Looking back later and going over your diary can lead to revelations you might not have come to otherwise. In your diary, you can express yourself, make goals, and record your spiritual visions and other experiences. Reading it later can lead to further revelations.

Happiness can be remembered by going over your diary periodically, and seeing your development. Good times can be remembered and appreciated. Also the negative aspects of your experience can be recognized and felt, and then healed when seen with detachment.

Memories and laughs with loved ones, lessons, tears, fears, and joy – you can learn a lot about yourself by writing down significant experiences for later review and additional understanding.

Amplify the Masculine or Feminine Energies

If you feel you are out-of-balance with regard to your masculine and feminine energies, visualize a color or a feeling that represents whichever one needs to be enhanced. Then feel or visualize that particular color. Imagine you are breathing it in and out for 20 seconds to 2 minutes.

Alternatively, visualize you are surrounded by the color/energy, breathe deeply, and then let go. The effects might not be instant, although in some cases they can be.

Chapter 10
THE MERKABAH AND THE MASTER'S JOURNEY

On the path to ascension, you might come across, see, or experience an aspect of your energy field take on a geometric form known as a *Merkabah*, or in the tradition of Jewish mysticism *Merkava*, which in Hebrew means *chariot*. We all have one. The Merkabah is a transdimensional vehicle, part of the Ascension process, and it allows us to access many realms.

The Merkabah is the living light aspect of who we are, an organic, natural aspect, our photon robe of light, which is the part of us that is made in The Creator's image. It's our chariot, our connection to the Godhead and through it we can experience the many mansions. There are no limits to where or how far we can go with it.

The Merkabah manifests as counter-rotating fields of light in the shape of two interlocked tetrahedrons in which one point of the tetrahedron points up and the other points down, forming the shape of a star tetrahedron.

THE MERKABAH

The top could be seen to represent the masculine, the fire element, and the sun; whereas, the lower represents the feminine, the Earth element, water, and the Earth itself. There are many interpretations, but it is our heavenly chariot, our gown of light. As all is holographic in nature, and when we are on The Ascension path we reunite in a conscious and coherent way with our Godhead Cell of Source through our Merkabah.

When delving into the Merkabah practices, light can appear around you during the activation stage of the advanced levels, which can be it starting to be seen in this realm and/or from other intelligences in theirs. Experiences related to the Mind's Eye such as telepathy can happen. Many abilities start to be unlocked beyond what we consider the norm – although actually they are normal.

For me, the Merkabah just appeared one day in a vision, and it wasn't until later that I realized what it was.

Most of my personal experience with this comes from my interactions with the Elohim and a whole host of different intelligences. Over time, I have come to the point of realizing that in these higher states of consciousness, whether in a Merkabah or remote viewing, we are not really going anywhere; our consciousness is, and this makes it appear as if we are. In this state, we go where we focus on going; in other words, we go by thought. To understand this is to go beyond the linear mind and the current scientific understanding of consciousness, and directing our actions and being responsible.

The Merkabah is something I have been in, and many of the Beings I have interacted with have fully activated their Merkabahs and are traveling in them across the many universes and dimensions. Sometimes, they even take passengers or create vehicles from consciousness.

Some of the ships we see in the sky are actually intelligences (Beings) in their Merkabahs. They can make their Merkabahs look like material objects such as triangular or saucer-shaped crafts. In some cases, they have been built and they are physical. This I can attest to. All of this is not black or white; the grey area in our knowledge is vast.

When we see a Being in a Merkabah blink out of range of our perception, it means the Being in it has full understanding of the operation of the Merkabah vehicle and can go beyond it and into a wave function. Then, through thought, the Being can navigate the universe. This means they can disappear and reappear anywhere, anytime in an instant.

It was explained to me by Metatron, the Elohim, and Michael through a download that some Beings can break down into an electron and travel in this way, because all electrons have a symbiotic relationship. The next stage is to do it through the photon because it and all is holographic in nature. Do with this information as you may.

Many techniques are out there for activating your Merkabah. But the effects of this need to be taken very seriously, as health and mental issues can arise if not done from the right place of love and rising to the occasion. Being responsible with this knowledge and the actions you take is also required.

Once you raise your frequency, you can start to operate from a geometric blueprint, which can change. From a triangle to a dodecahedron or to a Merkabah, many forms can come into your awareness. It just depends on your level of consciousness as to which geometric forms appear around you.

Some try to fully activate the Merkabah the first time they tap into it, but the truth is it can take many lifetimes – although sometimes it can be done in one. It depends on your love, level of consciousness, and being in truth. In terms of fully activating your Merkabah, I am talking about it appearing in the physical world around you, not just ethereally or in the Mind's Eye. Using it as an astral device can be done, but that's in the early stages of activating and working with it.

Some Beings we see traveling in the sky (or in our physical dimension) are made of light. They exist within the structure of their Merkabahs, although mostly we see the projection from within it, not the structure itself. The Rainbow light phenomena can be a by-product, too. In looking at images of Jesus, a circular glow like a rainbow can be seen around him. This is exactly what the Tibetans depict in their artwork. I have seen this myself with some of the intelligences I've observed.

It can take many years to realize the Merkabah, and in some cases, lifetimes of work. Intention, inner development, and self-mastery are key. Working with the Merkabah needs to be considered seriously because it can be harmful for those who have not evolved sufficiently in self-mastery. They can burn out or go insane. This is why I advise people to work naturally with the Merkabah and with the proper intentions.

A balance of science, wisdom, and understanding the mechanics of the body, as well as being spiritually open and being one with The Creator are needed in order to unlock this experience. Pure intentions and a loving heart help unlock knowledge of the Merkabah subconscious, and bring forth the Ascension journey.

Development, knowledge, and use of the Merkabah goes back to Atlantis, Lemuria, and Egypt, and off-world to the Pleiadians, Sirians, Arcturians, Andromedans, Lyans, and Orions, plus many others local, afar, and beyond our realm. Images of it are painted on Tibetan Mandalas and it is also represented in the Star of David. The photon, which has been captured in photos in recent years, if looked at three-dimensionally resembles the Merkabah, although when photographed in its original state it looks like the Knights Templar Cross.

Biblical References

Ezekiel 1

Psalm 68:17: The chariots of God are twenty thousand, even thousands of angels: the Lord is among them as at Sinai, in the holy place.

Psalm 104: 1-4: (1) Bless the Lord, O my soul. O Lord my God, thou art very great; thou art clothed with honour and majesty. (2) Who coverest thyself with light as with a garment: who stretches out the heavens like a curtain: (3) Who layeth the beams of his chambers in their waters: who maketh the clouds his chariot: who walketh on the wings of the wind: (4) Who maketh his angels spirit; his ministers a flaming fire.

2 Kings 2:11 And it came to pass, as they still went on, and talked, that, behold, there appeared a chariot of fire, and horses of fire, and parted them both asunder; and Elijah went up by a whirlwind into heaven.

Self Mastery – The Path to Ascension

To keep it simple, when discussing something as advanced as the Merkabah Light Body, ask yourself how you can be a vehicle for Source to work through. How can you be of service? What can you do to bring joy into the lives of others and yourself every day?

I have been given other techniques, but they are a bit lengthy and will be taught in future workshops. I hope to make this knowledge available in 2023 and beyond. Without consciously knowing it, if you have been practicing the exercises in this book you are already working on the Light Body and attaining your Merkabah Light Vehicle.

Moving towards Ascension is not complicated, but patience is needed and it takes time and effort. There are many other ways to grow spiritually out there, but I have always been shown the simple and most effective ones.

Once you start activating your Merkabah, you will need to tune into it regularly and connect to it, spin it, and work with it, even if only for a few minutes a day. Once you get to the point of thinking of it as a friend, you are at the point you don't have to tune in so much because it is working. The key is doing a Clearing beforehand, being in a state of love, and connecting to The Creator within you. It's all about intention and thought.

Exercises – Tips and Tools

Merkabah Light Vehicle Meditation

This is a simple exercise and there are a few ways to go about it. However, if you have been doing this work for some time, it might have come to you naturally during meditation in the form of a vision. Simply follow these instructions

1. First, do a Clearing.

2. Set an intention to connect to your Merkabah Light Vehicle.

3. Breathe loving energy in, and then breathe out any tension; repeat until you feel relaxed.

4. Breathe the loving energy in and out until you feel ready to move on.

5. Next, if not seeing your Merkabah Vehicle, use your imagination to visualize it. The Vehicle might appear in front of you, if so,

project your consciousness inside of it, or you might already find yourself inside of it. Either way, spin the top and bottom in opposing directions, and reunite with it through intuition. Your intuition is the Higher Self coming through to assist you with the mechanics of this process.

Chapter 11

ASCENSION AND BEYOND

After I went to bed one night in 2022, I awoke in a place with rainbow energy all around me. It was like a river.

A Being in a white robe with a golden chest and stomach piece appeared before me. He had long white hair, a beard, and a staff in hand, and he told me through thought with loving authority, "Remember how to travel the universe." The Being and the place seemed familiar.

Through an inner knowing, I was prompted to think of a place, and flash, we would appear where I was thinking. From the Egyptian pyramids to places I know from on and off-world from multidimensional experiences, these places I thought of and we would appear at them – just from thought.

After playing with this ability, what I believe to be a natural ability, we appeared back in the realm of the flowing rainbow energy.

Next, off in the distance I could see golden temples, one obelisk with a pyramid in front of it, and two domes on each side surrounded by smaller domes and structures.

As we approached these structures, we walked on what seemed to be a golden paved walkway which turned into a ramp walkway until approaching an opening where this walkway went to.

Walking further with the Being, we came to an opening, and when we walked in I saw many Beings sitting down gathered there. They looked at us and welcomed us with smiles, and they seemed surprised.

A feeling of rejoicing I felt in myself, as it hit me that these Beings were many saints, sages and Masters, not just from the Earth, but from the many mansions, worlds, and realms.

Then I woke up and a golden light was shining brightly about five feet off the ground near the wall to my right. At this point, I sat up in bed.

It was what I can only describe as a golden tablet about two and a half feet wide by about one and a half feet high. It lit up the whole room. I was now physically awake, like I am writing this right now. It was no dream.

Script of a familiar, yet unknown language etched into this tablet appeared. Then, the script changed to more script, and the same rainbow energy in the realm with the man appeared.

It was coming from the tablet straight to my head. A wave of intense, indescribable energy came with it. I felt like I was receiving a massive amount of information from it.

I turned my head and body away from the tablet, and the flow of energy stopped.

Something in me had to look back at it again, and the flashing script on the tablet started happening again with the rainbow energy coming at me, it was almost like turning pages in a book a million miles an hour, but the script was just appearing, almost like ten pages a second. With the rainbow energy coming from the tablet at my head, it was like a river of energy and information downloading into my human mind.

Quiet came over me as the script stopped appearing, the rainbow energy stopped flowing, and the tablet imploded on itself.

A darkness I was in now, sitting on my bed. Bewildered by what had just happened, a feeling of bliss came over me. After what seemed like a dream and then waking up in this physical world with the shining golden light in my room, to then seeing the tablet, I asked myself, *What just happened?*

I got out of bed, turned on the light, and walked into the lounge-room to light incense and do my morning prayer and give thanks and gratitude for everything I have received from The Creator, and for being a vehicle for Source to work through.

Putting on the kettle to make myself a coffee in the kitchen in the wee hours before sunrise, like I always do, I sat and wondered, *Who was that man, what just happened, and why?*

I have come to a place of acceptance after things like this happening for many years now. This is where I am these days when things like this happen. But this was more extreme and blissful than most of my experiences. There was something special about it, but I can't put my finger on it.

In the future I expect more will come to light about who, what, and why this experience happened. I have an idea, but I can't quite admit it to myself.

What was the script? I researched online straight away but couldn't find anything like it. I continued to wonder about the man and the Beings, who were gathered there. I knew some of them and had met them. But where was the place, what did the rainbow energy mean, why in the early hours of the morning, and why me?

Over the years, my experiences have been more like talking to a fellow human here on Earth in the waking state, even if it is through thought transfer. This new experience has left me with many questions I don't yet have answers to.

The feeling of love, bliss, and awe was beyond my other experiences with otherworldly Beings and the greater family of man. It was different.

Over time, I have come to learn that all our experiences are about us independently, but there's a catch to it. The catch is about having an experience and being led to how we can play our part in assisting the collective, as well as directives for going down our individual paths and having the experiences we are meant to have.

This is just a glimpse of what I can share from experience and knowledge at this time. My advice is to follow your heart and let the journey unfold. Surrender and go with the flow, and don't forget to look at the fruit from the information you receive.

Know also there is always a place beyond Ascension.

We are each at our own stage of evolution within the Mind of God, so embrace your growth, live every day to the fullest, and enjoy the nature of the human experience. Our true "home" is just a thought away and the universe is your playground – and you are already home.

My wish for you, who are reading this book, is that your path to Ascension is fruitful and filled with bliss. Know that all will be revealed in the Rainbow Light and that I will meet you one day in the Light, which is the Light of God's Mind.

BOOKS BY PETE

The Book of Shi-Ji

The Book of Shi-Ji 2

The Book of Shi-Ji 3

The Book of Shi-Ji 4 - Ascension

Connect to your Spirit and ET Guides

CE-5 Initiating Contact with Extraterrestrials

Awakening: UFOs and Other Strange Happenings

Operation Starseed: A Temporal War

ABOUT THE AUTHOR

Peter Maxwell Slattery is an international bestselling author, speaker, spiritual advisor, and educator who assists seekers with spiritual development, self-discovery, connection to Spirit Guides, soul family, purpose, and finding balance and joy in the Earthly experience and the God within.

His ability to teach is based on his own experiences and what he has learned from physical and non-physical contact with extraterrestrials, ultra-terrestrials, teachers, and Spiritual Masters.

Pete Slattery is certified/trained in meditation and hatha, kundalini, and tantric yoga. He is also a Reiki Master and trained in Yi-Gong, Qi-Gong by various teachers, and he has a certificate in counseling.

As a facilitator of many Eastern disciplines, multidimensional mind, and connecting to the God within, Pete now assists those who seek to awaken the Master within.

Teaching many worldwide to meditate, remote view, and initiate contact with extraterrestrials has led Pete to create a new center: Jaya Sanctuary in Victoria Australia.

He has appeared on the History Channel's *Ancient Aliens* and *Paranormal Caught on Camera*, Channel 7's *Prime News*, and *Sunrise*, and many other international television programs. He has made worldwide news, been in numerous documentaries, been written about in magazines, and has been a guest on mainstream radio shows, including Coast-to-Coast AM. Pete is also a musician and, as a filmmaker, he has made a number of documentaries on the subject of ETs. He was featured in *The Cosmic Secret*, which was a number one documentary film on iTunes in 2019, and James Gilliland's *Contact Has Begun 2*. Also, his UFO footage was featured in *Close Encounters of The 5th Kind*, which was also a number one film on iTunes in 2020. His most recent documentary is *Multidimensional,* released in 2021.

Pete's Websites:

petermaxwellslattery.com

ecetiaustralia.org

jayasanctuary.com

WATCHING THE SKY
Jessica Bryan

Crossing the bridge from Hood Canal, Oregon into Washington, I felt a lifting of energy, a shift. Everything was brighter and sparkling. The trees seemed greener and more alive.

We were twenty miles from Trout Lake and ECETI Ranch, founded by James Gilliland to study UFOs and other paranormal activity in the area around Mt. Adams. My primary purpose for making the trip was to meet Peter Maxwell Slattery, a world-famous UFOlogist from Australia who was visiting The Ranch. I had recently worked on three of his books. These books were "channeled" through Pete by "Shi-Ji," a Light Being from the star cluster Pleiades.

Mind you, I went with no expectations regarding UFOs or alternate realities, but I was hopeful I would see something unusual during "Skywatch Weekend."

It was quite cold the day we arrived, so we took long, hot showers. Afterwards, I decided to sit alone in the shower room for a while and enjoy the warmth. Closing my eyes and falling into meditation – which for me is more like a clairvoyant trance – I had a vision of the large field in the center of The Ranch. This field is where the human visitors sit at night to watch the lights in the sky, and also the lights going in and out of Mt. Adams.

In my vision, the entire field was filled with different colors and inter-dimensional Beings. They appeared to be having a party, a meeting. They were laughing and singing and dancing. In the center of the field an "elevator" reached from the ground up into the sky as far as I could see. Everything appeared as scintillating light.

On the left, some Beings were floating gently downward. Arriving at the party, they were greeted by those already in the field. On the right, others were floating upward, apparently leaving the "party."

According to my travel companion, the "elevator" is a "portal," a point of intersection between our physical reality and other worlds.

This vision was magical and indescribable, although some might say the Beings in my vision were coming and going to a "mother ship." I had heard other visitors at ECETI talking about the enormous

Self Mastery – The Path to Ascension

extraterrestrial ships that sometimes appear over the field, and also the other worlds and dimensions that connect to Earth in the ECETI field. Another way to explain this psychic phenomenon is that the UFOs and the Beings who inhabit them are in the same space as we are – but they are in an alternate universe that vibrates at a higher frequency.

I cannot explain this experience, not even to myself, nor do I understand it completely. I merely accept it as a beautiful experience of a peaceful, loving, compassionate presence, a vision of a happy place.

The next day, I met Pete Slattery, who also seems to vibrate at a higher frequency, even higher than some of the great gurus and teachers I've meet – but in a different way. Like most of the people I met at The Ranch, Pete is fully heart-centered and focused on service to humanity.

On Saturday night, I braved the cold and sat at the edge of the field for Skywatch with about thirty others. Pete and James Gilliland had laser pointers, and they would flash them up into the sky and shout, "There's one! (Referring to a UFO.) And, "WOW, look at that one power up." Everyone was cheering and laughing. I loved it!

My view of reality and the planet we live on was forever changed when Pete handed me his night vision goggles to watch the sky. I could hardly believe how much was going on above me. I observed several bright lights cross the sky and then blink off abruptly. There were also brilliant lights going in and out through apparent openings on Mt. Adams.

I feel profoundly changed by my experiences at the ECETI Ranch. I'm more centered in myself, and I'm hopeful for the future of humanity and Planet Earth. It really did seem, at least for a few days, that we are not alone in our struggles and that unconditional love is available to all life forms on all worlds and in all dimensions.

More of Jessica's writing can be found on her website:

www.theflowofgrace.net